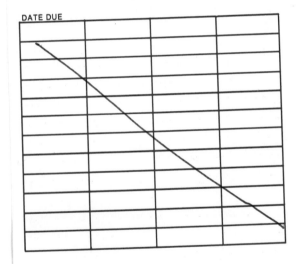

JAMES BOSWELL
and his world

DAVID DAICHES

JAMES BOSWELL

and his world

CHARLES SCRIBNER'S SONS
NEW YORK

Frontispiece:
Caricature of James Boswell by Sir
Thomas Lawrence.

Printed in Great Britain
Library of Congress Catalog Card Number 75-29826
ISBN 0-684-14549-9

Parliament Close, Edinburgh, from the Cowgate. On the fourth floor of one of these tall old buildings James Boswell was born in 1740.

JAMES BOSWELL was born in Edinburgh on 29 October 1740 in the fourth storey of one of those tall old tenements in Parliament Close in which his father, Alexander Boswell, had his Edinburgh residence, conveniently near to the law courts where, as a member of the Faculty of Advocates since 1729, he practised. Alexander Boswell was to become Sheriff-Depute of Wigtownshire in 1748, Lord of Session in 1754 and Lord of Justiciary in 1755. After the union between England and Scotland of 1707, Scotland lost its separate Parliament but it preserved its own legal system as it preserved its national Church. The Sheriff-Depute (who in practice called himself simply 'Sheriff' as after 1747 he was legally allowed to do) was the chief local judge of a Scottish county. A Lord of Session was a judge in the Court of Session, Scotland's supreme court in criminal causes, dating from 1732: its fourteen judges (Senators of the College of Justice, also known as Lords of Session) were presided over by a fifteenth, the Lord President, and sat in the old Parliament House, Edinburgh. Six of the Lords of Session constituted the bench of the High Court of Justiciary, presided over by the Lord Justice-Clerk, who was also one of the fifteen Lords of Session. These judges on appointment took the non-hereditary title of 'Lord' prefixed to the name of their estate; thus Alexander Boswell on his appointment as a Lord of Session became Lord Auchinleck after the name of his family estate in Ayrshire.

It is appropriate to introduce Boswell with reference to Edinburgh, the law, and a family estate in Ayrshire, because all three were to be intimately bound up with Boswell's sense of his own identity, with his satisfaction in being a member of an old Scottish landed family, his combination of pride in and resentment of his father's important position in the socially and intellectually dominating world of Scots law, and his combination of affection for his ancient native city and hostility to what he considered its narrowness and provinciality. Boswell was trained as a lawyer; his profession throughout his adult life was that of advocate (the equivalent of the English barrister); and the law determined the pattern of his career at almost every turn. In the Scotland of his day the law was the road to almost every kind of preferment. Edinburgh society was dominated by its legal members; historians, antiquarians, philosophers and writers as well as politicians nearly all came from the ranks of the law. The survival of Scotland's national legal system after Scotland's union with England in 1707 made that system in some respects a symbol of Scottish nationhood.

The Parliament House, Edinburgh. After the Union of Scotland with England this became the seat of Scotland's supreme criminal court, the Court of Session, of which Boswell's father was a member.

Judges of the Court of Session in 1808. Members of the Court were at the apex of Edinburgh society.

Judges formed the apex of a legal community which itself formed an Edinburgh aristocracy. Peter Williamson's first *Edinburgh Directory* (for 1773–74) ranks the citizens in this order: Lords of Session, Advocates, Writers to the Signet (a select order of 'writers' or solicitors), Lords' and Advocates' Clerks, Physicians, Noblemen and Gentlemen, Merchants, and so on. Boswell prided himself on coming from a Scottish family of consequence.

The Boswells of Auchinleck had been landed proprietors since the fifteenth century and took part in many of the violent activities that characterized Scotland's turbulent history without any special distinction, but several of James Boswell's ancestors married into the nobility – two indeed brought royal blood into the family by marrying connections of the Scottish royal house. Boswell throughout his life was very conscious of these connections and considered himself socially the equal of almost anybody. 'Tell me if I can be a worthy Scots laird,' he concluded the sketch of his life he wrote for Rousseau when he was twenty-four, indicating his early ambition to play his part with pride and distinction on his ancestral Scottish estate. This ambition was from an early age counterpointed against his ambition to perform on a wider stage, to be known and admired in London and indeed in Europe. He felt both proud of his Scottishness and restricted by it. The paradox was common among eighteenth-century Scottish gentlemen. The union of 1707 had brought feelings of frustration and national humiliation at the loss of Scottish national identity and a consequent defensive reassertion of Scottish pride which led to a wave of interest in Scottish antiquities, folklore and history; it also brought, somewhat later, an ambition among Scottish intellectuals – the *literati*, as they called themselves – to assert themselves before the world as British writers using a pure English idiom, thus demonstrating that Scots could beat the English at their own game and make at least as great a contribution to British culture as their southern neighbours. The *literati* were on the whole rather ashamed of their distinctive Scottish speech and tried, at least in their writings, to purge their language of 'Scotticisms'. Boswell had his moods of fierce Scottish patriotism, especially when provoked by anti-Scottish feelings encountered in England, and many times he looked back to the days when Scotland was a proud and independent kingdom and regretted the union 'with the warmth of an ancient Scot' (as he told Rousseau in 1764); but at the same time he tried strenuously to acquire a southern English accent and was more and more drawn to London as a cultural centre beside which Edinburgh – even the Edinburgh of the *literati* and the Golden Age of philosophers, historians and scientists – was narrow and boorish.

Alexander Boswell was a less complex character than his son: he was an old-fashioned patriotic Scottish Whig in the pre-1707 tradition, for whom King William had been the saviour of a Protestant Scotland, and the established Presbyterian Church of Scotland represented the only proper Scottish way to worship. He remained untouched by the Anglicizing tendencies of the *literati*, proudly spoke his native Scots on the bench, and was more than content with his dual position as laird in Ayrshire and legal luminary in Edinburgh. Born in 1707, the very year of the union, he had studied law at Leiden, as his father had done before him and as so many Scotsmen did in the late seventeenth and in the eighteenth centuries, for Scots law, like Dutch law and unlike English law, was based on Roman law, on which Dutch jurists were experts. He was a good Latinist and a conscientious and hard-working sheriff and judge. He was also a good friend and neighbour on his Ayrshire estate, where in 1762 he built the fine neo-classic Auchinleck House with a motto from Horace's *Epistles* (about a well-balanced mind finding content) carved on the front.

Boswell's mother was born Euphemia Erskine, daughter of Lieutenant-Colonel John Erskine, Deputy Governor of Stirling Castle and through him great-granddaughter of John Erskine, second Earl of Mar (1588–1634) whose second wife, Colonel Erskine's grandmother, was a daughter of that Duke of Lennox who was cousin of Darnley, father of James VI of Scotland and I of England. Both Euphemia and her husband Alexander claimed descent from the second Earl of Kincardine (he as grandson, she as great-granddaughter) and his Dutch wife, Veronica van Aerssen of the distinguished Sommelsdyck family. Euphemia was the daughter of her father's old age, born to his third wife; she was brought up in seclusion

by her maternal grandmother and developed into a delicate and pious young woman of gently sentimental religious views. Boswell as a youngster seems to have regarded her as a source of affectionate protection, in striking contrast to his blunt and demanding father who always seemed to threaten to crush his personality. Alexander Boswell had high ideals of truthfulness and public service. James recollected later having got 'a hearty beating' from his father for lying, and 'having truth and honour thus indelibly inculcated upon me by him', but this beating seems to have been an isolated case (which is probably why it impressed itself so forcibly on Boswell's memory). Alexander was not a cruel man, but his temperament was quite different from his son's and they were never able properly to understand each other. He believed in hard work and duty and lacked any trace of gaiety though he was possessed of a kind of ironic humour, which he was to demonstrate often at his son's expense and which on at least one occasion he displayed on the bench: when an Italian musician in Edinburgh was prosecuted for firing on a man who tried to enter his house at midnight to visit his daughter, he pleaded in his defence that he thought the man was a *fur nocturnus*, a nocturnal thief, to which Lord Auchinleck replied, 'I believe he was not a *fur nocturnus*; but I believe he was a *furnicator*.'

Boswell's parents: Alexander Boswell, Lord Auchinleck, and his wife, Euphemia.

View of Edinburgh from the north, before the building of the New Town.

The Edinburgh into which Boswell was born had not yet expanded under the influence of the elegant neo-classic ideas of civic planning which were to produce the New Town, though the expansion proceeded apace in Boswell's lifetime. The Edinburgh of his child-hood was still essentially the dirty and noisy medieval city built along the ridge that runs from Edinburgh Castle to the Palace of Holyrood-house. When the Jacobite Rebellion broke out in 1745, the little boy (as he later told Dr Johnson) 'wore a white cockade and prayed for King James, till one of his uncles (General Cochrane) gave him a shilling on condition that he would pray for King George, which he accordingly did'. But when the Highlanders occupied Edinburgh in September and October 1745 the Boswell family were probably not in the city, since the court terms were from 12 June to 11 August and from 12 November to 11 March: the family had in any case spent that summer at Newington, then a quite separate area to the south of the city. But it was in Edinburgh that Boswell started school in 1746, at James Mundell's private academy in the West Bow, an old and history-haunted street where the notorious warlock Major Weir lived until he was judicially strangled and burned in 1670. 'For upwards of a century after Major Weir's death' (wrote Robert Chambers in 1822) 'he continued to be the bugbear of the Bow, and his house remained uninhabited. His apparition was frequently seen at night, flitting, like a black and silent shadow, about the street. . . . Some people occasionally saw the major issue from the low close at midnight,

The Netherbow Port, Edinburgh.

mounted on a black horse without a head, and gallop off in a whirlwind of flame.' The little Boswell must have listened with a fascinated horror to these stories, which may well have been the beginning of his lifelong obsession with capital punishment and public executions.

Mundell's school had a good reputation and many of its pupils distinguished themselves in later life. But Boswell was unhappy there, and at the age of eight he was taken away to be educated by private tutors. The reason for the change may have had nothing to do with Boswell's unhappiness, for it came about the time of the death of his paternal grandfather, when his father inherited the family estate at Auchinleck and would want to have his family with him there when the courts were not sitting at Edinburgh. Shortly before his father's death Alexander Boswell was appointed Sheriff of Wigtownshire, which required his residence in the sheriffdom for four months of the year, though he appears not to have taken his family with him during his periods of residence in Wigtown. The great Boswell authority Professor F. A. Pottle believes nevertheless that as a small child Boswell must have seen his father laying down the law as Sheriff and that this indelibly impressed on his mind a picture of him as the stern judge handing out punishments to offenders.

As a child Boswell was timid and delicate, with what he later described as a 'melancholy temperament'. He was afraid of ghosts, afraid to go out alone in the Edinburgh streets at night, 'terrified by everything I did not understand'. His mother, in spite of the gentleness of her piety, taught him the Calvinist doctrines of eternal punishment, which terrified him, and though she believed in the efficacy of Divine Grace, to whose operations she entreated her little son to yield, this only seems to have made matters worse. Fortunately, his first tutor, a twenty-five-year-old aspiring minister named John Dun, set him to reading *The Spectator* and helped him to acquire his 'first notions of taste for the fine arts and of the pleasure there is in considering the variety of human nature', and, in matters of religion, played down the terrors of Hell and emphasized the beauties and joys of Heaven. He also taught Latin well and helped young Boswell to read Latin poetry with understanding and real enjoyment: all his later life Boswell would quote readily from Horace and wrote grammatically accurate Latin prose with fluency.

In 1752 Alexander Boswell presented John Dun to the parish of Auchinleck (having as laird the right to appoint the minister), and James and his younger brother John got a new tutor, Joseph Fergusson. (His second brother David was only three at the time. An elder sister Euphemia had died when he was three months old.) Fergusson, who though in his early thirties was still unsuccessful in his search for a parish, was an altogether harsher teacher than Dun, and Boswell found him completely uncongenial. What may have started as a psycho-somatic response to Fergusson's method of teaching developed into a genuinely serious illness. ('I preferred being weak and ill to being strong and healthy,' Boswell admitted to Rousseau, for when he was well his 'slavery would begin again'.) Among the symptoms of his illness was a profound depression, which would naturally have disturbed his father because of the strain of melancholy and even of madness in his heredity. James's paternal grandfather had been subject to black moods and obsessive fancies, and of his father's two younger brothers one was mentally unstable and the other eccentric in matters of religion almost to the point of lunacy. And Boswell's younger brother John may have already displayed some of the symptoms which were to develop into prolonged gloom with periods of violence as a result of which he would spend nearly all his adult life in confinement.

Boswell was sent for a cure to the watering-place of Moffat, then a small village with none of the amenities of the famous English watering-places but popular for its sulphur springs. It is in the northern part of Dumfriesshire, in lovely Border country, with the Tweedsmuir Hills to the north and St Mary's Loch to the north-east. The country-side, the springs (he both drank and bathed in the water) and the company seem to have combined to restore his health. Both his melancholy and his 'scorbutic' symptoms disappeared and he recovered his appetite. Henceforth we hear no more of his delicate health, though he was to remain subject to bouts of acute depression.

It was just about the time of his thirteenth birthday that Boswell entered Edinburgh University for the session of 1753–54. Generally known as the town's college and officially designated *Academia Jacobi Sexti*, the College of James VI (who had founded it), the university still occupied the old college buildings that had been begun in 1581: the new building on the same site (now known as the 'Old Quad'), designed by Robert Adam and completed much later after the modified design of W. H. Playfair, was not begun until 1789. Thirteen, or more usually fourteen, was a common age of entrance to the University in Boswell's time. Much of the teaching was conducted in the form of drilling and interrogating of the kind associated today with more elementary kinds of education. The first degree, as in all Scottish universities to this day, was the Master of Arts, though many students did not bother to take the degree but attended individual courses according to their preference. Boswell certainly took classes in Latin (in which he was already well drilled), Greek (which he now started from scratch, and never got far with) and Logic, which was taught by John Stevenson, who first introduced Locke's philosophy to Scottish students. George Stuart, his Latin professor, was competent but unimaginative; Robert Hunter, his Greek professor, does not seem to have been able to impart much Greek to any of his students. But Stevenson was a great success with the students. Alexander ('Jupiter') Carlyle, who had entered the University in 1734 – Stevenson had been appointed in 1730 – wrote of him enthusiastically in his *Autobiography*: 'I went to the Logic class, taught by Mr. John Stevenson, who, though he had no pretensions to superiority in point of learning and genius, yet was the most popular of all the Professors on account of his civility and even kindness to his students, and at the same time the most useful; for being a man of sense and industry, he had made a judicious selection from the French and English critics, which he gave at the morning hour of eight, when he read with us Aristotle's *Poetics* and Longinus *On the Sublime*. At eleven he read Heineccius' *Logic*, and an abridgement of Locke's *Essay*; and in the afternoon at two . . . he read to us a compendious history of the ancient philosophers, and an account of their tenets. On all these branches we were carefully examined at least three times a week . . . all of us received the same impression – viz., that our minds were more enlarged, and that we received greater benefit from that class than from any other.' 'No man', said a later writer, 'ever held a Professor's chair in the University of Edinburgh who had the honour of training up so many young men to the love of letters.' His influence on Boswell was powerful and permanent.

Boswell probably also attended other Arts classes, including Mathematics, Natural Philosophy (Physics) and Moral Philosophy. He then proceeded to take classes in Botany, Astronomy and Roman Antiquities, the last being relevant to his study of Roman Law on

Alexander 'Jupiter' Carlyle.

which, with other legal studies, he was now also embarked. Altogether he attended classes at the University for six years.

It was at Edinburgh University, about the time of his sixteenth birthday, that Boswell met two people whose friendship was to mean a great deal to him. The first was John Johnston, a Border Scot some ten years older than he, distinguished by his elegant clothes, his warm heart, his love of Scottish history, and his willingness to be dominated by the so much younger Boswell. The other was William Johnson Temple, an Englishman born in Berwick-on-Tweed in 1739, destined for a career as an Anglican vicar and a minor essayist, future friend of the poet Thomas Gray, at this time a pious and conscientious young man of considerable charm. Boswell at this time was himself shy, conscientious and self-doubting, and found Temple's friendship immensely reassuring. They both loved, and discussed, literature, and they took walks together in the countryside around Edinburgh talking about everything under the sun. Temple introduced Boswell to the Church of England chapel in Carrubber's Close, thus encouraging his disenchantment with the sterner Presbyterian mode of worship and his love of religious ceremonial.

Boswell, as he later informed Rousseau, was now tortured by sexual desire and was horrified lest he would 'sin and be damned'. Sexual anxieties, among others, led to melancholia. He became, he says, a Methodist, and then, on a second visit to Moffat, to cure his melancholia, met a mystical Pythagorean sheep-farmer named John Williamson, who turned him to vegetarianism and a belief in metempsychosis. His mental and emotional instabilities were exacerbated by Stevenson's lectures on metaphysics, which set him brooding on the problem of determinism and free-will, and the insolubility of the problem completely unsettled him. The country was now plunged into the Seven Years War (1756–63), and at first Boswell, in his own words, 'wished to go among the Highlanders to America' (the Black Watch, the Highland regiment formed in 1739, sailed for America in April 1756), but his father put a stop to that. Altogether Boswell seemed to his father to be behaving with disturbing irrationality. But all the time he was developing, and growing in confidence, coming, it would seem, to regard his tendency to melancholia as evidence of his originality and interestingness. We know virtually nothing of his last year at the University (1757–58), but when it is over he emerges as gay, confident, amorous and a versifier. We hear no more of his Pythagorean beliefs.

Boswell's first published verses, written in May of the same year, appeared in the *Scots Magazine* for August. Entitled *An Evening Walk in the Abbey-Church of Holyroodhouse*, they are in the eighteenth-century tradition of broody 'graveyard' blank verse: they reveal him as an imitator of some facility, but nothing more. Throughout his life Boswell would periodically break into verse, generally light verse that

Sir David Dalrymple, who became a Lord of Session as Lord Hailes in 1766. He was both man of law and man of letters, and his patronage encouraged Boswell's first literary steps.

could be lively and occasionally witty, but, though he made his début as a writer in this medium, he had no more than a scribbler's talent in it. This early versifying, and its recognition by publication in the company of well-known poets of the day, was good for his self-confidence, which was now encouraged by the friendly patronage of Sir David Dalrymple, fourteen years his senior, who was to become a Lord of Session as Lord Hailes in 1766 and was historian, antiquary, essayist and general man of letters as well as jurist, and the much older Lord Somerville, a man of ancient Scottish lineage and vast literary acquaintance, patron of the Edinburgh stage. The stage was still under attack in Edinburgh, especially from the more rigid elements in the Church; the fight for the establishment of a legal theatre in the city had been going on with varying fortunes since 1715 and was not to end until the official licensing of the Theatre Royal in 1767 (when Boswell wrote the prologue for a play entitled *The Earl of Essex*, in which he deplored the 'mistaken zeal, in times of darkness bred', which had prevented the legal establishment of a theatre earlier). Before this the device used to get round the law was to present a play gratis at a concert-hall after the performance of a concert or some other legal entertainment. West Digges, Edinburgh's leading actor at the time of Boswell's first involvement with players, took over the management of the Canongate Concert Hall or Playhouse, and would announce his productions in this form: 'Concert Hall in the Canongate. Will be presented gratis (after the several Concerts), the following Dramatic performances: . . . ' In 1758, when Digges was

Mr Clench and Mrs Yates as the Duke and Duchess of Braganza in *The Tragedy of Braganza*, by Henry Crisp, which they played to great applause in Edinburgh in 1785 even though, according to Jupiter Carlyle, Mrs Yates was often 'more than half-seas-over'. Boswell had a lifelong passion for the theatre.

riding high, young Boswell, having emerged from the 'mixture of narrow-minded horror and lively-minded pleasure' at the thought of what was going on in the Canongate to a single-minded concentration on the lively-minded pleasure, began attending plays regularly and tried to model himself on the gallant and handsome Digges.

Yet this newly confident young Boswell, consorting with actors and actresses, writing verses, and for a while thinking of marrying an eighteen-year-old heiress called Martha Whyte, was far from decided on what his own character was or ought to be. He was constantly looking for other characters on whom to model himself, and this was to be a prominent characteristic of his for many years to come. He wanted to be like this man or like that man, according to mood and circumstance, now admiring someone's assurance, now someone's gravity and sincerity, now someone's quiet self-control, now someone's extrovert swagger. This chameleon element in Boswell was bound up with his sympathetic curiosity about people, which was to stand him in such good stead as a biographer. He was genuinely interested in the details of other people's personalities, in the revealing gestures or throw-away observations which illuminated their mental and emotional furnishing. And it was not just objective curiosity: somehow, he thought this knowledge would help him to be himself. At the same time he was also looking for a father-figure to replace his own father whose inability to communicate with his son, or to respond in any acceptable way to his son's signals of emotional need, led him to seek other older men with whom he could enter a relationship of almost filial discipleship.

He was on his own in Edinburgh now. Until 1758 he had lived in his family's Edinburgh home during the academic year and was in Auchinleck with the family during the courts' summer vacation, but in April and May 1758 the family were at Auchinleck with the Edinburgh house closed, and Boswell was in lodgings in Edinburgh. It was a gay interlude of playgoing and scribbling. Then the following autumn he started the serious study of the law and settled down for a while to industrious habits, which lasted until the following spring. In the spring of 1759 he was on his own again, more passionate than ever about playgoing. He fell head-over-heels in love with an actress, Mrs Cowper, and wrote rhapsodical reviews of her performances in the Edinburgh press of the summer of 1759. He became a Freemason, being admitted on 14 August to the Canongate Kilwinning Lodge (the same lodge of which Robert Burns was to be assumed a member in 1787). Some rumours of his son's swaggering and gallivanting must have reached Lord Auchinleck's ears, for after Boswell had joined his family at Auchinleck in September his father abruptly told him that he was not to return to Edinburgh University on the imminent opening of term, but would go instead to the University of Glasgow, which meant living in a city without the temptations of theatres, actresses and seductive literary friends.

Sixteen years earlier Alexander Carlyle had gone from Edinburgh University to Glasgow. 'One difference I remarked between [Glasgow] University and that of Edinburgh,' he wrote, '. . . which was, that although at that time there appeared to be a marked superiority of the best scholars and most diligent students of Edinburgh, yet in Glasgow, learning seemed to be an object of more importance, and the habit of application was much more general.' Glasgow was a sober town of Presbyterian merchants, rapidly growing in wealth through its trade in sugar and tobacco with the West Indies and the American colonies: in January 1746 its unromantic Whig citizens had given a freezing welcome to Bonnie Prince Charlie and his Jacobite army. Carlyle reported that 'there never was but one concert during the two winters I was at Glasgow, and that was given by Walter Scott, Esq. of Harden, who was himself an eminent performer on the violin; and his band of assistants consisted of two dancing-school fiddlers and the town-waits'. But on the academic side at least Glasgow had much improved since Carlyle's day; chief among its luminaries was Adam Smith, appointed Professor of Moral Philosophy in 1752, who lectured not only on that subject but also on Rhetoric and Belles Lettres. Boswell heard both courses of lectures, the former of which contained the germ of *The Theory of Moral Sentiments* (1759) and the *Inquiry into the Nature and Causes of the Wealth of Nations* (1776). The lectures on Rhetoric and Belles Lettres were published (as reported by a student in 1762-63) only in 1963. Boswell enjoyed these lectures particularly, with their breaking free from the old formal rhetorical categories and

Adam Smith, author of *The Wealth of Nations* and Professor of Moral Philosophy at Glasgow, to which University Boswell was sent by his father to remove him from the temptations of Edinburgh.

lively references to authors both ancient and modern. He rejoiced at Smith's observation that we are glad to know the most minute details about the lives of great men (such as that Milton wore latchets instead of buckles on his shoes) and must have agreed, too, when Smith talked of the great fault of generalization in describing character, to avoid which 'there ought to be always some particular and distinguishing circumstance annexed'.

It was in February 1760, while he was living in lodgings at Glasgow and attending Glasgow University, that Boswell published (in London) what appears to have been his first book, *A View of the Edinburgh Theatre during the Summer Season, 1759, containing an Exact List of the Several Pieces represented, and Impartial Observations on Each Performance*, a collection of reviews he had contributed the previous summer to *The Edinburgh Chronicle*. The fifty-page pamphlet was attributed to 'a Society of Gentlemen'. But though the work was anonymous, Boswell was already known as a friend of the theatre, as is testified by the warm dedication to him in the same year of Francis Gentleman's adaptation of Thomas Southern's play *Oroonoko*. So in theatre-less Glasgow Boswell was clearly dwelling nostalgically on the delights of the Edinburgh stage. He was apparently also dwelling on the delights of Mrs Cowper, or at least responding to her influence. Mrs Cowper was a Roman Catholic, and, on being made aware of Boswell's revulsion from the Presbyterian mode of worship in favour of more richly traditional rituals, she had put him in touch with her priest in Edinburgh who gave Boswell some works of Catholic apologetics. Boswell responded with zeal, in spite of the fact that Roman Catholics at this time were still under severe legal disabilities, disqualified from entry into the Church, the Army and Navy, the Universities and Parliament, and (in strict law but not always in practice) even from succeeding to an estate. Catholic places of worship were tolerated, so long as the congregations were small and private and did not publicize themselves. In moving towards Roman Catholicism Boswell was moving away from everything expected of him and planned for him by his father and his friends. When at the end of February 1760 Boswell wrote to his father that he was about to embrace Roman Catholicism and even become a monk or priest, the horrified Lord Auchinleck at once summoned his son to Edinburgh. Boswell's reply, on 1 March 1760, was to take horse for London. There he found his way to a Roman Catholic bookseller in Drury Lane who put him in touch with a priest at the Bavarian Chapel. He was duly received into the Roman Catholic Church and planned to retire to a French monastery.

Boswell was clearly in a mood of high exaltation. He was in revolt against the drabness of his Glasgow life, the strictness and lack of colour in Presbyterian worship, and the world of stern Whiggery represented by his father. The appeal of Roman Catholic worship

In 1760, when Boswell embraced the Catholic faith and his first prostitute, casual fornication was an accepted subject for comic prints. This one is captioned 'The Old free method of Rouzing a Brother Sportsman'.

to him was more aesthetic than theological. At the same time as he was planning what amounted to a sacrifice of all his material prospects and an entry to the monastic life, he was immensely excited by London and all the delights it offered. He made contact with a pimp (a fellow Scot) as well as a priest, and within a short time of embracing Roman Catholicism he embraced Sally Forrester in the Blue Periwig, Southampton Street (off the Strand), his first prostitute, who initiated him into 'the melting and transporting rites of love'. Lord Auchinleck, whom Boswell had kept informed of his address, through wisdom or by chance took the best possible course to wean his son away from the joys of aesthetic asceticism he saw in the Church of Rome. He enlisted the help of his fellow Ayrshireman Lord Eglinton, a worldly and pleasure-loving peer now living in London, who sought Boswell out and instructed him fully in the delights of London. As Boswell put it,

Eglinton freed him 'from the gloom of superstition, although it led [him] to the other extreme'. Or, as Pottle has summed it up, 'Eglinton rescued Boswell from religious error by making him a libertine, in every sense of the word.' We must not forget, however, that Boswell by his curious mixture of aesthetic religiosity and sensual excitement at the prospects afforded by London made such a resolution fairly easy.

Eglinton introduced Boswell to the Duke of York, an undiscriminating young rake whose royal title nevertheless enchanted Boswell, who wrote a set of verses about the 'Royal Youth's' openness with him and the unfortunate gulf fixed between their stations. He also met Laurence Sterne, who had suddenly become a celebrity after the publication of the first two volumes of *Tristram Shandy* the previous year, with the result that for some years preposterous imitations of the Shandy style erupted periodically in Boswell's own prose. And, under Eglinton's influence, he gave up the idea of either a religious or a legal career and decided on a commission in a Guards regiment. Such a commission needed either political influence or a lot of money, and preferably both. Boswell wrote to his father asking him to buy for him a commission in a regiment of Foot Guards not on active service but stationed in London or near by. Surprisingly, instead of refusing outright Lord Auchinleck came up to London to see if he could use his influence with the Duke of Argyll to get Boswell the commission he desired. Boswell was presented to the Duke and made a good impression, but nothing came of the meeting. Auchinleck begged his son to come home with him and think the whole matter over carefully. At the end of May they returned together to Scotland.

Boswell spent some years vainly pursuing his ambition of obtaining a commission in a Guards regiment not on active service abroad. He liked the idea of the uniform, the gay social life, the social prestige, that went with the life of a Guards officer in London. It is at this time that his passionate addiction to fine clothes first becomes conspicuous. Years later he was to note in his journal that 'dress affects my feelings as irresistibly as music'.

With his son back in Scotland, Lord Auchinleck offered to obtain him a commission in a marching regiment, but Boswell wanted none of that. It must be the law then, Auchinleck insisted, which did not necessarily mean an active career as an advocate, because in the eighteenth century law was regarded as a liberal education for a gentleman and would have been considered an appropriate background for a laird living on (and off) his estate. 'The Gentlemen who are styled Advocates in this country', wrote an English visitor to Edinburgh in 1774, 'are almost innumerable; for every man who has nothing to do, and no better name to give himself, is called Advocate. Of those, however, who practice and get business, the number is extremely few; . . .' Auchinleck offered to teach his son law himself, and for about two years he appears to have done so. This was in

Edinburgh, where Auchinleck spent much of the year and where Boswell was now living in sullen resentment with his family. He went out when he could and, with London's glittering attractions ever in his recollection, tried to approximate them in whatever Edinburgh could afford by way of convivial meetings, playgoing and wenching. He had acquired his first dose of gonorrhoea in London, and now he got another and more severe infection which necessitated treatment lasting four months.

He continued to write verse and publish pamphlets. In November 1760 he published a pamphlet containing observations on a comedy by Samuel Foote which had recently been produced in Edinburgh; the title-page did not give Boswell's own name but had the words 'by a Genius', which was not wholly self-mockery but gave the reader the chance of thinking it so while at the same time asserting his own hope that he was somebody special and different. The pamphlet contains some blatant Shandyisms and some evidence that Boswell had read Samuel Richardson and profited from his way of describing the smallest details of human gesture and behaviour. In August 1761 he published a pamphlet containing two poems and a long introduction consisting of commendatory letters, two by himself (one, ironic in tone, signed 'J.B.', and another, wholly serious, said to have been written by the author of the poems in submitting them to the publisher), one signed 'G.D.' and another signed 'A.E.'. The last two are jovially burlesque in style; they were written by two men who had now become Boswell's close friends, George Dempster, twenty-nine-year-old advocate and recently elected Member of Parliament for Perth burghs, and Andrew Erskine, member of a talented and distinguished Jacobite family, of the same age as Boswell. The poems themselves are feeble; the presentation of them in this odd way shows what was to become increasingly a Boswell characteristic – the determination to be known in one way or another, preferably as a genius but if that were not possible as a clown.

In the summer of 1761 the Irish actor Thomas Sheridan (father of the dramatist) gave two series of lectures on Elocution and the English Tongue, in an Irish brogue, at St Paul's Chapel, Edinburgh. At a charge of a guinea a head three hundred gentlemen attended the series over a period of four weeks, and then Sheridan gave a shortened two weeks' course for ladies and for those gentlemen who had been unfortunate enough to miss the first course. The main course of lectures was attended by Boswell and his friends Erskine and Dempster, all anxious to rid themselves of their Scotticisms and speak standard English. Sheridan was sponsored by the Select Society of Edinburgh, believing, as they announced in a document published soon afterwards, that 'gentlemen educated in Scotland have long been sensible of the disadvantages under which they labour, from their imperfect knowledge of the ENGLISH TONGUE, and the impropriety with which

Lord Kames (left), with Hugo Arnot, the first historian of Edinburgh, and the eccentric Lord Monboddo. Born in 1695, Lord Kames was something of a father-figure to Boswell – one of several in his life.

they speak it.' It was characteristic of the state of mind of the Edinburgh *literati* that they could, like Boswell, combine pride in being Scots with a belief that their spoken speech represented a shameful corruption of the English tongue. But Boswell's state of mind was more mixed even than this, for it was complicated by the conviction, formed on his first visit to London, that, proud member of an old Scottish family as he was and frequently asserted himself to be, he really belonged in the English capital of wit, fashion and pleasure.

Boswell adopted Sheridan as a father-figure, and confided all his trouble to him. When Sheridan returned to London Boswell wrote him at length about all his doubts and problems, and Sheridan replied in kindly fashion. He was to meet Sheridan many times on later visits to London. He also began a mutual burlesque correspondence with Erskine, with an eye on eventual publication. The pattern was to become a familiar one in Boswell's life: lively younger men as companions in exhibitionism, an older person as confidant and moral model.

In September 1761 Boswell published in *The Scots Magazine* a letter, by 'A Gentleman of Scotland to the Earl of ***' who was quite clearly the Earl of Eglinton, in which he dwelt with reminiscent pleasure on the good times he had had in London under Eglinton's tutelage and looked forward to a return visit. The letter is a pure piece of showing off (no one could have had any doubt about the identity of the author, since he gave so many details), a reckless snapping of his fingers in the face of the sobrieties represented by his father. He mentioned in the letter that he might well be about to be married to a beautiful young lady. Nothing came of this, or of any of the other marital prospects he flattered or amused himself with in rapid succession at this time. In December 1761 he published (still anonymously) an *Ode to Tragedy*, which he had the effrontery to dedicate to James Boswell, Esq. In the autumn of 1761 he contributed thirty poems to the second volume of Alexander Donaldson's *Collection of Poems by Scotch Gentlemen*. In March 1762 he published in London, himself guaranteeing the costs, a poem entitled *The Cub at Newmarket*, a humorous narrative of his own humiliation at the Jockey Club at Newmarket where he had gone from London with Eglinton and had been left isolated and awkward. He dedicated this rather silly performance to the Duke of York, without permission, which made both the Duke and Eglinton very angry: the resulting quarrel with Eglinton meant the end of Eglinton's help in getting Boswell a commission in the Guards.

Thomas Sheridan tried to find a compromise between the opposing views of Boswell and his father about the former's career by suggesting that Boswell be called to the English Bar, but, to Boswell's surprise and anger, Lord Auchinleck would not agree. He turned in his troubles to another father-figure, Henry Home, Lord Kames, who had become a Lord of Session in 1752 and became a Lord of Justiciary in 1763; he was now sixty-five years old and a distinguished scholar, literary critic and agricultural improver. 'Boswell', wrote Kames in 1761, '(for how many qualitys good and bad does that name bundle up together!) I hear your friend Capt. Erskine is in Edinburgh at this precious moment. I long to see the outlandish monster that soars beyond an Eagle and is yet tame like a dove; that can sting like a Serpent and yet lull you into Pleasure like a Syren. Will you shew him here this Evening?' The tone is familiar, teasing, affectionate: Kames clearly liked both young men. By the end of 1761 Boswell was on regular visiting terms with Kames. He was also on more intimate visiting terms with the actress Mrs Love, wife of the actor James Love who was Boswell's friend. She seems to have fallen readily enough into Boswell's arms, and he seems to have used her for sexual relief when no more seductive girls were available. One such girl has been identified with virtual certainty as Kames's married daughter Jean, who had married Patrick Heron when she was seventeen and despised her husband. Heron was to divorce her in 1772 for adultery with an army officer. When Boswell met her she was only recently married, but already prepared to engage in a passionate physical affair with him. He was not easy about it, feeling guilty with respect to her father and unhappy at the idea of adultery with a woman of his own class. Jean had fewer qualms. 'I love my husband as a husband,' she told Boswell, 'and you as a lover, each in his own sphere. I perform for him all the duties of a good wife. With you I give myself up to delicious pleasures. We keep our secret. Nature has so made me that I shall never bear children. No one suffers because of our loves. My conscience does not

The Earl of Eglinton, who introduced Boswell to some of London's more raffish pleasures, such as that symbolized by the print below, entitled 'Love in a window'.

Engraved by E.Finden.

24

reproach me, and I am sure that God cannot be offended by them.' Meanwhile Lord Auchinleck, disgusted with his son's style of life in general, was talking darkly of disinheriting Boswell and selling Auchinleck.

By early 1762 Boswell was enjoying the favours of both Mrs Love and Mrs Heron, as well as of a 'curious young little pretty' called Peggy Doig, probably a servant girl, who bore him a son the following December. He received a mild reprimand from the kirk treasurer, to whom he paid the requisite fine (such things were handled more gently in the city, and by gentlemen, than in the country, where peasant offenders would have had to mount the cutty stool), had the baby christened Charles, found him a foster-mother and provided money for his maintenance. Charles died in the spring of 1764, when Boswell was in Holland: Boswell had been in London when the baby was born, and as he went directly from London to Holland he never saw him.

In July 1762, when he was having supper with Lord Kames, Boswell received a message from Lord Eglinton saying that he was in Edinburgh and would like to see him. Boswell, still hurt, sent back a cool reply that he would call in the morning. Kames cheered Boswell by saying that Eglinton's influence was not necessary: he should go to London with an increased allowance from his father and a recommendation from his father to the Duke of Queensberry, who would surely use his influence on Boswell's behalf. Boswell proceeded to snub Eglinton the next morning, and Eglinton got the message.

Boswell kept at his father: he wanted permission to go to London and pursue his attempt to get a commission in the Guards. As he had worked well at his law studies, in spite of his other activities, and passed the private examination in Civil Law on 30 July 1762, Lord Auchinleck finally assented, and it was agreed that Boswell would go to London in November. In a flurry of high spirits he agreed to join Kames in a tour of the Border counties before leaving for London, visiting among other places the Kames estate at Kirroughtrie, Kirkcudbrightshire, in south-west Scotland. The trip is especially memorable for any biographer of Boswell, for it produced the first of his remarkable and invaluable journals, the 'Journal of My Jaunt, Harvest 1762'. The Journal was written for John Johnston and a more recent friend William McQuhae, who had succeeded Joseph Fergusson as tutor to the Boswell family and was only three years older than Boswell. The fact that it was meant specifically for their eyes deprives it of some of the utter candour that makes so many of his other personal records so extraordinary – for example, he is very cagey in talking about Jean Heron, with whom he managed secret meetings both at Kirroughtrie and at Dumfries – but it lacks nothing in vivacity and in that wealth of observed detail, that specificness of gesture and conversation, that is so characteristic of Boswell as a

(*Opposite*) James Boswell as a young man about town. 'Dress', he noted later in his Journal, 'affects my feelings as irresistibly as music.'

Arthur's Seat – 'that lofty romantic mountain on which I have so often strayed in the days of my youth'.

diarist. He can communicate the precise flavour of a particular social gathering; selects the exact anecdote that reveals the character both of the teller and of the person of whom it is told (e.g. David Hume heard from Garrick why Johnson declined ever again to go backstage in the theatre: 'I will never come back. For the white bubbies and silk stockings of your Actresses excite my genitals'); evokes a casually met character by describing his costume, his accent, his wig; realizes a scene dramatically by judicious selection and verbatim presentation of dialogue; describes his own behaviour and conversation and changing moods with unabashed egotism; shows a never-flagging interest in himself and others. One evening he read aloud to the company some of Dr Johnson's essays and noted that he differed from Kames, Adam Smith and Hugh Blair about the 'Author of *The Rambler*. They will allow him nothing but Heaviness, weakness and affected Pedantry. Whereas in my Opinion Mr. Johnson is a man of much Philosophy, extensive reading, and real knowledge of human life.' He was soon to find in Johnson his most permanent and influential father-figure.

Boswell returned to Auchinleck and then to Edinburgh, where his father arrived on 8 November, having recently learned that his second son John, now an Army lieutenant, was mentally deranged and confined in a Plymouth hospital. The following Sunday he attended

the English (Episcopalian) Chapel, had dinner with Lord Somer,
ville, spent some time with West Digges and had supper with Kames.
He spent the next morning talking with his parents. 'They were very
kind to me. I felt parental affection was very strong towards me, and
I felt a warm filial regard for them.' Well he might, for Lord Auchinleck
had promised to pay Boswell's debts and allow him £200 a year.
At ten o'clock he got into his chaise and set off for the south. 'As I
passed the Cross, the cadies [messenger boys] and chairmen bowed
and seemed to say, "God prosper our noble Boswell."' Drawn
though he was by the magnet of London, he was still very much
aware of his Scottish patriotism. He 'made the chaise stop at the foot
of the Canongate' then 'walked to the Abbey of Holyroodhouse,
went round the Piazzas, bowed thrice: once to the Palace itself, once
to the crown of Scotland above the gate in front, and once to the
venerable old Chapel'. He then stood in the court before the Palace
and bowed three times to Arthur's Seat, 'that lofty romantic mountain
on which I have so often strayed in the days of my youth, indulged
meditation and felt the raptures of a soul filled with ideas of the
magnificence of God and his creation'.

Boswell was in London from 19 November 1762 until 6 August
1763, when he left for Holland. He kept a vivid and revealing journal
of his stay in London which he wrote up at irregular intervals from

brief memoranda jotted down daily, and sent in weekly instalments, with a letter, to John Johnston. Frank though it is, the journal, being intended for Johnston's eyes, does not always tell everything (it is, for example, reserved about his relations with his father), and the biographer often finds that the original scrappy memoranda, which also survive, are more informative about the exact progress of Boswell's moods and ideas. It is the liveliness of the journal, its precise evocations of scenes and characters and conversations, that appeals most to the modern reader. Boswell here reveals himself unmistakably as an uncannily gifted observer and recorder. He continued to keep a journal for most of his life, but the London Journal, though not containing his most mature and perceptive writing, is unparalleled in its freshness and its verbal sparkle.

Boswell travelled to London by post-chaise, spending nights *en route* at Berwick, Durham, Doncaster and Biggleswade. When he had his first view of London from Highgate Hill he 'was all life and joy' and burst into song. He at once got in touch with his friend West Digges, who recommended that Boswell should stay at the Black Lion, Water Lane, Fleet Street, while looking for permanent lodgings, which he eventually found some days later in Downing Street. He agreed to pay forty guineas a year for his three rooms in a family house, dining with the family when he wished at a shilling a time, but shortly afterwards was able to get the rent reduced to £30. His allowance from his father was £200 a year (£25 every six weeks) and he had to work out a fairly strict budget.

He called on a number of Scottish friends and acquaintances in London, searched in vain for Sally Forrester at the Blue Periwig, and on his first Sunday in London attended Mayfair Chapel, Curzon Street, where he heard a fine sermon and 'thought that God really designed us to be happy'. He called on James Dodsley, the bookseller and publisher, and collected thirteen shillings due him for *The Cub at Newmarket*. He completely made up his quarrel with Lord Eglinton, dining with him often during his stay in London and persisted against all the probabilities in hoping for his influence in obtaining a commission in the Foot Guards, which was one of the main reasons for his coming to London at all. By 25 November he was 'really unhappy for want of women' and picked up a girl in the Strand, though on this occasion he did not pursue the matter to a conclusion, which he often did on later occasions, several times picking up a prostitute in nearby St James's Park and engaging with her on the spot. He generally reproached himself for such 'low' sexual activities and made resolutions to have more genteel affairs. He was constantly afraid of contracting venereal disease and for this reason preferred, when he was with a prostitute, to employ 'armour' (a prophylactic sheath). He dined out, visited the theatre, beefsteak-houses and coffee-houses, talked, listened, observed, bubbled, had alternating moods of high excitement

and deep depression, tried to control and adjust his character according to constantly changing ideals, and was determined to get his commission in the Guards and stay in London.

Drury Lane Theatre.

He also continuously speculated about his own nature. One
Sunday, during divine service, he was surprised to find himself
'laying plans for having a woman' while having 'the most sincere
feelings of religion'. He concluded that he had 'a warm heart and a
vivacious fancy'. Visitors from Scotland stirred the ambiguity of his
Scottish feelings. 'For to see just the plain *hamely* Fife family hurt my
grand ideas of London.' He often recorded his unease at hearing Scots
spoken by compatriots. Yet he remained a proud Scot and, during
this period of Lord Bute's prime ministership when Scots were
particularly unpopular in London, fiercely resented any anti-Scottish
feeling he met. Once at the theatre when the mob began to abuse two
Highland officers in the audience, his 'Scotch blood boiled with
indignation' and he jumped on the benches and swore violently at the
demonstrators. He was capable of absurd as well as violent speeches
while waiting with a theatre audience for the play to start: on one
notorious occasion he entertained the audience by his skilful imitations
of a cow. He noted that at times when he despaired of being the
dignified figure he wanted to be, he was content to 'lower [his] views
and just to be a good-humoured comical being'. At other times his
mind regained 'its native dignity' and he 'felt strong dispositions to be
a Mr. Addison'. A mixture would perhaps be best: 'Mr. Addison's

Farmyard imitations while waiting
for the play to start.

David Garrick as Ranger, in *The Suspicious Husband*, produced at Covent Garden in 1747.

character in sentiment, mixed with a little of the gaiety of Sir Richard Steele and the manners of Mr. Digges.'

On 2 December Boswell waited upon the Duke of Queensberry, one of the most influential Scotsmen in England, in the hope of enlisting his influence in his Guards scheme, but his sanguine hopes from this quarter ended on 26 December with the receipt of a letter from Queensberry saying that he could do nothing. He paid court to the Countess of Northumberland for the same purpose, but though she was kind to him in the end came the usual disappointment and frustration. He tried every possible way of getting appropriate influence used on his behalf, and gave up his hope of a commission in the end with great reluctance. At the same time he kept his options open. While he was 'pushing to get into the Guards', he recorded in December, with the object of distinguishing himself and getting promotion (but really with the object of wearing a handsome uniform and living in London), he realized that, even if unsuccessful in his hopes, he was at least 'seeing the world, studying men and manners, and fitting [himself] for a pleasing, quiet life in old age, by laying up agreeable ideas to feast upon in recollection'. He could then 'enjoy a serene felicity at the delightful Auchinleck, the ancient seat of a long line of worthy ancestors'.

He renewed his acquaintance with Thomas Sheridan, now living in London, forming a relationship with the forty-three-year-old Irishman that moved from real affection (for Sheridan's genuinely warm nature) to irritation (at his somewhat dogmatic views and his lack of enthusiasm for Boswell's own verse). He renewed his friendship with Andrew Erskine, now a lieutenant in the Seventy-first Foot, soon to go on half-pay with the disbanding of his regiment, and with George Dempster, now a Member of Parliament for Forfar and Fife burghs: the three spent many a gay evening together. He got to know David Garrick and was absolutely delighted when on 20 January 1763 Garrick expressed not only his friendship but also his admiration for Boswell, saying 'Sir, you will be a very great man.' 'What he meant by being a great man I can understand,' Boswell recorded complacently. 'For really, to speak seriously, I think there is a blossom about me of something more distinguished than the generality of mankind.' Boswell compared Garrick with the other actor Thomas Sheridan, greatly to the former's advantage, and from then on professed real love for him.

In some ways the most extraordinary relationship Boswell formed at this time was that with the lady he calls in his Journal Louisa, whose real name was Mrs Anne Lewis. She was an actress long separated from a 'harsh, disagreeable' husband, having discovered that the marriage was not legal, quite well educated and genteel in manner and conversation. In successive calls on her Boswell gradually established an intimate relationship and found himself more and more in love.

His plan was to make her his mistress, so that (as he noted after the affair was over) he could enjoy 'at least a winter's safe copulation'. He lent her two guineas when she was pressed for a debt, and steadily established himself in her good graces until in January she yielded to him. Several times during the next week he was 'permitted the rites of love with great complacency', though the complacency seemed somehow to diminish his passion. Then, only a week after his first sexual encounter with her, he felt the symptoms of gonorrhoea, which soon became unmistakable and severe. He must have got it from Louisa, though she had assured him that she had no other intimates. She had lied to him, deceived him and infected him, he decided, in considerable anguish of mind. He called on her on 20 January and coldly reproached her with her conduct; she defended herself with pale earnestness and almost convinced Boswell that she had been unaware of her own infection. But his surgeon had told him she must have been aware of it, so he put her behaviour down to 'the grossest cunning' and left her with exaggerated formality. On 3 February he wrote her a bitter letter, pointing out that the 'little sum' he had lent her was neither payment for prostitution nor a charitable gift, and asking her to return it. On 10 February a packet containing the money and nothing else was left for Boswell at his lodgings. He never saw Louisa or heard from her again. Had he misjudged her? He could never be certain, and could only resolve to 'think no more of the matter'. Meanwhile, he had to keep indoors for the most part for five weeks until he was cured. He was visited by friends, who cheered him up, and employed much of his time in reading, going through David Hume's *History of England*.

On 5 January Boswell was agreeably surprised by the arrival of his younger brother John 'in good health and spirits'. John was now a lieutenant in the Thirty-first Regiment of Foot, and had recovered from his mental illness. His recovery proved to be temporary, and though the two brothers met a number of times during Boswell's stay in London and got on well together, John was soon to relapse into the mental illness which was to dog him all his life. That evening Boswell dined, as he often did, with Lady Betty Macfarlane, sister of Andrew Erskine: he was fond of her but despised her elderly and parsimonious husband. He reproached himself in his Journal for his clowning behaviour at dinner: people might applaud him at the time, 'but behind his back hold him very cheap'. This is a characteristic reminder to himself. On 19 January Boswell, Dempster and Erskine attended the first performance of David Mallet's tragedy *Elvira*, which they determined to damn. Boswell was deeply prejudiced against Mallet for having changed his good Scots name of Malloch to a name that could be considered English. The three young men decided to produce a pamphlet attacking the play, which duly appeared later in the month and though it was generally ill received Boswell looked

forward to getting 'much fame and much gold' by writing books and pamphlets. On 7 February he wrote a lively letter to Eglinton protesting that he (Boswell) was a man of genius and writing the obituary he hoped for, which described James Boswell as an amiable man who improved and beautified his paternal estate of Auchinleck, distinguished himself in Parliament, commanded a regiment of Foot Guards, 'and was one of the brightest wits in the court of George the Third'. But he had his period of black melancholy too, exacerbated when his 'sad distemper' asserted itself. But on 27 February he considered himself cured, and revelled in a 'sweet elevation of spirits' at the thought of going freely about London again. 'Pray remember,' he wrote to himself in his memorandum of 6 March, '... how happy you now are in the full enjoyment of liberty. Summer will come when all Scots will be gone. Then you'll grow more English and fine.' His thoughts turned confidently to the Guards again. But he also continued to have intermittent moods of the deepest depression.

His old friend Temple turned up in London in April, and they had many meetings in the subsequent months. Eventually, after Boswell had quarrelled with his Downing Street landlord, Temple, who had left for Cambridge, lent Boswell his lodgings in the Inner Temple, where Boswell stayed happily from 7 July until his departure for Holland. On 3 May he went to the Tower of London in the disappointed expectation of seeing the notorious John Wilkes leave: he went on to Newgate and saw some condemned criminals, and the

An execution at Tyburn.

(*Opposite*) Temple Bar. This famous gateway, dividing Fleet Street from the Strand, stood before the Temple, where Boswell lived in borrowed lodgings for just under a month in the summer of 1763.

(*Right*) Samuel Johnson, whom Boswell met at Thomas Davies's bookshop (*below*). 'I shall cultivate this acquaintance,' Boswell noted in his Journal.

(*Overleaf*) The Journal entry, in Boswell's hand, describing the historic meeting.

next day, urged by a horrid fascination, went to Tyburn to see their execution, which threw him 'into a very deep melancholy'. Boswell met John Wilkes on 24 May, at the house of the writer Bonnell Thornton, and Wilkes was cordial to him. But by this time he had already had a more momentous meeting, the most important in his life.

On 16 May he had been drinking tea in the parlour behind Thomas Davies's bookshop in Russell Street when, about seven in the evening, the great Samuel Johnson came in. The scene is described in the Journal and was to be worked up, in a classic and memorable account, in Boswell's *Life of Johnson*. The fifty-four-year-old Grand Cham of literature overpowered Boswell with crushing wit when he tried to excuse his Scottish origin (for he knew of Johnson's prejudice against Scotland) and crushed him again when Boswell tried to curry favour with a remark about Garrick. But Boswell remained to remember and later note down the great man's conversation (the first of very many such occasions); Johnson grew less harsh and more civil to him; and Davies told Boswell after Johnson had left that it was clear that Johnson liked him very well. On 24 May he called on Johnson at his chambers in the Inner Temple and was cordially received and pressed to stay. 'Upon my word,' he noted in his Journal, 'I am very fortunate. I shall cultivate this acquaintance.' This was one resolution Boswell kept.

this morning with the illustrious
Donaldson. In the evening I went
to Temple's; he brought me ac:
:quainted with a Mr Claxton a
very good sort of a young man tho'
reserved at first. Mr Nicholes was
there too. Our conversation was
sensible & lively. I wish I could
spend my time allways in such company.

     Monday 16 chay.
Temple & his Brother breakfha:
:ted with me. I went to Love's
to try to recover some of the mo:
:ney which he owes me. But alas
a single guinea was all I could
get. He was just going to dinner,
so I stayed & eat a bit, tho' I was
angry at myself afterwards.
I drank tea at Davies's in Ruf:
:el street and about seven came
in the great Mr Samuel John:
:son, whom I have so long wished
to see. Mr Davies introduced
me to him. As I knew his mortal
antipathy at the Scotch, I said
                      to

to Davies; don't tell where I come
from. However he said From Scotland.
Mr Johnson said I indeed I come
from Scotland, but I cannot help
it. Sir replied he . That I find
is what a very great many of
your countrymen cannot help.
Mr Johnson is a Man of a moot
dreadfull appearance. He is a
very big man is troubled with sore
eyes, the Palsy & the King's
evil. He is very slovenly in
his dress & speaks with a
most uncouth voice. yet his
great knowledge, and strength
of expression command vast
respect and render him very
excellent company. He has
great humour and is a worthy
man. But his dogmatical rough:
:ness of manners is disagreable.
I

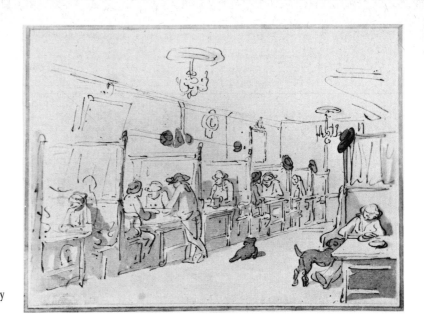

The Cock Tavern in Fleet Street, by
Thomas Rowlandson.

All this while Boswell's relations with his father were strained. They
had been corresponding with acerbity. In February Lord Auchinleck
wrote to Boswell of his displeasure with aspects of his conduct and
Boswell replied offensively. Auchinleck broke off correspondence
and spoke of selling the estate. Boswell then had a change of heart and
asked his and his father's friend, Sir David Dalrymple, to intervene,
but before he could do so Auchinleck decided to write a long and
patiently reasoned letter to his son. This letter, dated 30 May, was
received by Boswell on 8 June with great relief. Auchinleck, after
detailing Boswell's offences (including publishing the frivolous
correspondence between himself and Erskine and a general neglect of
his reputation), concluded by proposing a legal career with the prospect
of election to Parliament, so making his parents happy and adding
lustre to the family name. If he settled for this, Auchinleck would let
Boswell go abroad for a while. But if he were still bent on the army,
then he had better accept an ensigncy in a marching regiment (which
he had been offered) and, though Auchinleck did not like the idea,
he would approve provided that Boswell stuck to that career as his
'business for life'. But no more mimicry, journals, publications and
'acting without prudence and discretion'. Boswell called this 'a very
kind letter' and decided that he would give up his army scheme and
pursue the law after all. 'I considered that by getting into the plan of
civil life, I should have all things smooth and easy, be on a respectful
footing and of consequence in my own country, and please my worthy
father, who, though somewhat narrow in his notions, is one of the best
men in the world.' This was far from the end of Boswell's quarrels

with his father, but it marked a decisive point in his career. He wrote to John Johnston on 16 June that he had laid aside all thoughts of going into the army, disgusted with the 'neglect and hollowness' of the great people whose help he had sought. He added that he had asked his father if he could go abroad before returning to Scotland, and hoped to return from his travels 'a decent grave Man'.

He pursued his acquaintance with Samuel Johnson, calling on him on 14 June and spending an evening with him at the Mitre on the 25th, when he told Johnson his life story to which the great man 'listened with attention'. He told him of his strict religious upbringing, of his subsequent religious doubts and his resolution of them (although he was still not 'clear in many particulars'). Johnson, touched by the young man's confidences, cried, 'Give me your hand. I have taken a liking to you' and went on to strengthen his Christian faith with a variety of arguments. Boswell then talked to Johnson about his relations with his father, and received Johnson's sympathy and advice. Further meetings with Johnson followed. On 14 July they drank two bottles of port together at the Mitre, after which Johnson took Boswell cordially by the hand and said, 'My dear Boswell! I do love you very much.' Noting this in his Journal, Boswell added: 'I *will* be vain, there's enough.'

Unlike Auchinleck, Johnson approved of Boswell's keeping a journal, advising him to keep one all his life, 'fair and undisguised' (not that Boswell needed any such advice). Although since 'being honoured with the friendship of Mr. Johnson' he had 'more seriously considered the duties of morality and religion and the dignity of human nature' and 'considered that promiscuous concubinage is

In the Mall. Rowlandson's pen-and-wash sketches convey very well the atmosphere of the London Boswell knew.

The town of Harwich. Johnson and Boswell drove up the London road, *F*, by stage-coach when Boswell took ship for Holland

certainly wrong', he still indulged in intermittent bouts with prosti-tutes ('mean profligacy' was his term). On 22 July, in the Turk's Head Coffee-house, he complained to Johnson that he was 'much afflicted with melancholy, which was hereditary in [his] family' and Johnson said that he too had been greatly distressed with melancholy and took refuge in study and meditation. He told Boswell that 'he wished to visit the Western Isles of Scotland, and would go thither with [him] when [he] returned from abroad', adding that he took to few people as much as to Boswell. On 30 July Boswell and Johnson sailed down the Thames together to Greenwich, where they dined. On returning to London they supped at the Turk's Head, where Johnson said that he would accompany Boswell to Harwich, for it had been agreed between Boswell and his father that he should study law in Holland and set off from Harwich almost immediately. On 1 August he was tapped on the shoulder 'by a fine fresh lass' as he came up the Strand, and 'could not resist indulging [himself] with the enjoyment of her'.

The next day he wrote a memorandum to himself beginning: 'Set out for Harwich like Father, grave and comfortable. Be alert all along, yet composed. . . . Go abroad with manly resolution to improve, and correspond with Johnson. . . . See to attain a fixed and constant character, to have dignity.' On 3 August he supped with Johnson at the Turk's Head. Early on the morning of the 5th he and Johnson left London in the Harwich stage-coach. He was to remember the details of the scene and describe it in the *Life*. They dined together at Harwich, after Boswell had secured his passage in the packet-boat to Helvoetsluys and put his luggage aboard. Then they walked together down to the beach, 'where we embraced and parted with tenderness, and engaged to correspond by letters. I said, "I hope, Sir, you will not forget me in my absence." JOHNSON, "Nay, Sir, it is more likely you shall forget me, than that I should forget you." As the vessel put out to sea, I kept my eyes upon him for a considerable time, while he remained rolling his majestic frame in his usual manner; and at last I perceived him walk back into the town, and he disappeared.'

Boswell landed in Holland on 7 August and proceeded to Rotterdam, where he met a young Scottish merchant, Mr Archibald Stewart, who put him up at his house for a few days. Then he went to Leiden, where he spent some days, after which, in gloomy spirits, he set out for Utrecht in a *trek schuit*, a sort of covered barge. He became ever more melancholy during the nine hours' journey, and reached Utrecht in a state of the deepest depression. Holland seemed a gloomy

Leiden, which Boswell reached by canal barge, filled him with gloom and melancholy.

Rotterdam at the time of Boswell's visit: a view of the Haringvliet looking towards the English church.

and desperate place. He returned to Rotterdam 'in a condition' (he wrote to John Johnston on the 23rd) 'I shudder to recollect'. Archibald Stewart tried to cheer him up, but in vain. He wrote to Temple of his utter wretchedness, and Temple replied attributing his condition to idleness and exhorting him to play the part of a Man. This reply and his reading some relevant essays in *The Rambler* produced an improvement in his state of mind. He returned to Utrecht, engaged rooms in or owned by the Keizerhof inn on the Cathedral Square opposite the cathedral tower, hired a servant, an elderly Swiss called François Mazerac, started attendance on a course of lectures in Civil Law, and began a regular course of reading in Greek, Latin, French and English. He also summoned a tailor and ordered first 'a Leyden suit of green and silver' and then one 'scarlet with gold'. He made a note to himself to be mindful of his worthy father, guard against liking billiards, and to 'be easy and natural, though a little proud'. He continued to keep a journal, and though it has not been recovered we can reconstruct his life in Holland from his memoranda and from letters to and from him. In a letter to Temple on 23 September he professed to be thinking of Archibald Stewart's sister as a possible wife, but the notion soon 'evaporated'. He was to entertain a great variety of abortive matrimonial schemes before he finally married his cousin Margaret Montgomerie in 1769.

In spite of his resolutions, his determined embarking on his studies, his regular composition of passages of French prose and English verse, his grappling with Dutch, and a fairly full if somewhat stiff social life, Boswell was not happy in Holland. On 15 October he made out an

The City Hall, The Hague.

'Inviolable Plan to be read over frequently' in which he admonished himself to give up frivolity and idleness, to 'keep quite clear of gloomy notions which have nothing to do with the mild and elegant religion of Jesus' and keep this faith always firm, and to support the character of the future Laird of Auchinleck. He would eventually return to Scotland, become an advocate there, and perhaps enter Parliament; as an advocate, he could visit London every year and spend some months at Auchinleck 'doing good to your tenants and living hospitably with your neighbours, beautifying your estate, raising a family, and piously preparing for immortal felicity'. These pious resolutions of Boswell, which recur frequently in his memoranda, are not hypocritical. One side of his character did earnestly desire the kind of settled, respectable, socially acknowledged, gently pious existence he here looks forward to. Another side was restless, exhibitionist, excitable and unstable. Yet another side was tortured by doubts about religion and especially by uncertainty about 'a future state'. Each of these different sides was liable to come to the surface suddenly and unexpectedly.

His endeavour to suppress all but the first during his stay in Holland did not yield happiness. He got some comfort from making friends with two Scotsmen in Utrecht, the Reverend Robert Brown, pastor of the English-speaking Presbyterian church in Utrecht, and James Rose, Brown's lodger. 'Fight out the winter here, and learn as much as you can. Pray, pray be *retenu*' (an often repeated exhortation to himself), he admonished himself at the end of November. In December he sought bodily and mental refreshment in three weeks at The Hague where he was warmly greeted by his relative Heer van Sommelsdyck ('amiable, soft, genteel') and enjoyed a lively round of dinners, dances and sightseeing. On Christmas Day at the Church of England Chapel, after receiving permission from the Chaplain, he took the sacrament and 'was in devout, heavenly frame, quite happy'. It was the first time he had received communion in the Church of England. On 6 January he was presented to the young Prince of Orange, and the next day went to Leyden, thence to Rotterdam (where he reproached himself for having sat up all night playing cards) and then, 'quite happy', back to Utrecht on the 16th.

But soon he was fighting ennui and indolence, and though his life was temporarily enlivened by a passionate flirtation with the beautiful young widow Madame Geelvinck, the lady's departure for The Hague in late February left him in a thoroughly gloomy state. His gloom was deepened by learning in a letter from Johnston on 9 March that his little son Charles, whom he had never seen, had died. He had taken his parental role seriously and had 'formed many agreeable plans for the young Charles. All is now wrapped in darkness. All is gone.' His depression persisted, exacerbated by discussions with Brown and Rose about predestination. 'I have been tormenting myself with abstract questions concerning Liberty and Necessity, the attributes of the Deity, and the origin of Evil,' he wrote to Temple on 23 March. These themes haunted him all his life.

By now Boswell was curiously involved with the most remarkable woman in his life, Isabella Agneta Elisabeth van Tuyll, more familiarly Belle de Zuylen, who had given herself the literary name of Zélide. This twenty-three-year-old member of a distinguished Dutch family, an independent-minded intellectual who was conducting her own war against the stuffiness of Dutch life, both attracted Boswell by her mental liveliness and literary gifts and repelled him by what he considered her unwomanly freedom and independence of manner. He light-heartedly fancied himself in love with her as early as 31 October 1763, but in the immediately following months his references to her are more censorious than amorous. In spite of her being an heiress and an aristocrat, and thus a suitable person for him to consider marrying, Zélide deeply offended Boswell's concept of 'male dignity'. For Boswell had what would today be considered an extreme male chauvinist attitude to women: their function was to minister to his pleasure and comfort, and any evidence that they had character and intellect and dignity of their own disconcerted him. Throughout his four years' relationship with Zélide, Boswell treated her with insufferable condescension, always assuming that he had the right to reprove, advise, and prescribe for her, though in fact it was she who was the more intellectually distinguished. At the same time he was genuinely fascinated by her. This was the recipe for a strange, up-and-down relationship and it would take a book to follow its vagaries.

By January 1764 Boswell and Zélide were sufficiently intimate to analyse to each other the progress of their mutual feelings. On 6 February Boswell admonished himself to be 'modest and on guard' with her and on the 8th at a tea-party she 'roasted' him about his projected plan (never carried out) of a Scottish dictionary. He made a pact with her that they should be frank with each other for the whole winter. 'But' (he noted to himself in his memorandum) 'you talked too much. They all stared. Be on guard.' On 25 February she told Boswell he could 'see her at home at least once a week'. He added: 'This girl trusts you; like her. . . . Shun marriage.' On 17 April he wrote to Temple that Zélide was charming, was a *savante* and a *bel esprit* who had published some things. But – 'She is much my superior. One does not like that.' She would make a sad wife, he told himself the next day. But he could not get her out of his system. Her self-confessed hypochondria and lack of religion other than 'the adoration of one God' made Boswell fear that her mind was unhinged. 'Yet I loved her.'

The most remarkable woman in Boswell's life: Zélide, otherwise Elisabeth van Tuyll – a forerunner of women's liberation.

Four days before Boswell's departure from Utrecht the two began a correspondence (largely in French) which lasted four years. In a long letter to her of 9 July 1764 he writes that he is convinced that she has been in love with him and probably still is. 'If you love me, own it. I can give you the best advice.' His vanity provokes him to ask a further question: 'If I had pretended a passion for you (which I might easily have done, for it is not difficult to make us believe what we are already pleased to imagine) – answer me: would you not have gone with me to the world's end?' Understandably, Zélide did not reply, and only the following January, after Boswell had written protesting at her long silence, did she relent, and wrote an explanation of her silence. 'You went on repeating, ringing all the changes possible on the words, that I was in love with you, that my feelings were those of love. You would have me admit this, . . . I was shocked and saddened to find, in a friend whom I had conceived of as a young and sensible man, the puerile vanity of a fatuous fool, coupled with the arrogant rigidity of an old Cato.' Boswell, who had for several months been exchanging cordial letters with Zélide's father, wrote to Zélide defending and explaining himself. On 16 January 1766 Boswell wrote from Paris to Zélide's father making a formal proposal for Zélide's hand. It was not the fever of love, he said, but a steadier emotion that led him to propose 'a calm, conjugal engagement'. He would require an oath on Zélide's part that she would never see or correspond with anyone of whom her husband and brothers disapproved, and that she would not publish anything without their permission. He added an account of his ancestry, prospects and character ('singular and romantic, . . . made to give her infinite pleasure' but also a hypochondriac and suffering from 'an excess of self-esteem').

Monsieur de Zuylen replied that Zélide was still contemplating marriage with the Marquis de Bellegarde (who had long been pursuing her) so he could not put Boswell's proposal to her. When Boswell next wrote to Zélide he was telling her of his plan to marry someone else (one of many marriage plans that never came off). 'Well! So you once loved me! I wish you all the more success and happiness in the choice your heart makes at present.' On 26 February 1768 Boswell wrote from Edinburgh to say that his plan for marrying Catherine Blair had collapsed and he was still free. He and Zélide might still marry: he left the decision up to her. On 14 May he wrote to Temple that his pride and Zélide's vanity would never agree and he had written to Zélide to say so. In March Boswell sent Zélide his book on Corsica to translate into French; she wanted to make some changes, which he would not allow, and this offended her so that she abandoned the translation. In 1771 Zélide married M. de Charrière, her brother's tutor, and henceforth lived in seclusion in the manor of Colombier at Neuchâtel. In 1787, when she was forty-six, she fell in love with the nineteen-year-old Benjamin Constant, who eventually left her for Madame de Staël, after which Zélide became more of a recluse than ever. Her bid for a lively and independent intellectual life compatible with genuine love and friendship had failed, and the rest was silence.

In the midst of his varying feelings towards Zélide and his intermittent courting of Madame Geelvinck Boswell had his usual ups and downs of melancholy and exuberance, the former predominating. Letters from his father showed unusual understanding. 'I have the greatest feeling for you under these melancholy fits you are sometimes attacked with,' Auchinleck wrote on 2 April 1764, 'but for your comfort know that numbers who have been subject to this distress in a much greater degree have made a good and an useful figure in life.' The cure was to acquire as much knowledge as possible and avoid idleness. On receipt of this letter Boswell felt 'all well, all gay'. He admonished himself in his daily memorandum to 'lose not Plan' and appreciate his 'fine situation' in Utrecht. But he added: 'Think if God really forbids girls.' The next day he reminded himself that it was Holy Week. 'Be grave.' Two days later he was writing to Temple of a return of his gloomy distress. 'I have constitutionally a tender and a gloomy mind.' On a trip to Amsterdam in May he alternated between cheerfulness and gloom. He felt better at The Hague in early June, attending a gathering at the British Ambassador's on King George's Birthday 'in a genteel suit of flowered silk'. On the same day he received a letter from George Keith, Earl Marischal, the famous Jacobite who had been out in the Rebellion of 1715 and now lived in Prussia, saying that he would accompany Boswell to Berlin and one from his father sanctioning the trip and allowing him 'credit upon Berlin of £30 a month'. He was delighted. On 11 June he wrote

The Royal Palace, Berlin. Here 'Mr Boswell of Auchinleck' was received – but, to his annoyance, not by King Frederick the Great.

Temple: 'I look back to my late situation with fearful amazement, and scarcely believe that it has been.' What a strange man he was, he exclaimed, 'at one time an abject, perhaps an offensive, being; at another time the most spirited, the most agreeable of the sons of men'. He was no longer doubting the truth of Christianity. He wrote again on the 17th that he was 'quite free from hypochondria'. He left Utrecht in a coach-and-four on 18 June 1764 with the Earl Marischal and a new servant (François not wishing to leave Utrecht), the Swiss Jacob Hänni. As his spirits rose he reflected that he had been 'as chaste as an anchorite' since he left England and looked forward to 'fine Saxon girls, etc.'.

He paraded himself in Berlin as Mr Boswell of Auchinleck, a proud Scot of ancient lineage, and he was generously entertained by the local notabilities. He paid two visits to the Court of Brunswick, where he was entertained with dinners, visits to the theatre, 'grand music' and other experiences that 'supremely elevated' him. But though he planned and intrigued and cajoled and persuaded he was unable to fulfil his main object in visiting Berlin – to be presented to King Frederick the Great. He was received at the Court of Prussia, but not by the King. By mid-November he was tired of Berlin, and showed this by occasional ill-temper, which almost led him into a duel with an offended Frenchman. He left Berlin in late November to visit other small German courts, saw the graves of Luther and Melanchthon at Wittenberg (and, as he had promised, wrote to Samuel Johnson with the paper resting on Melanchthon's tomb), was impressed by the University of Leipzig, and kept searching among the German princelings for 'a prince of merit who might take

Jean-Jacques Rousseau.

a real regard for [him]'. Karl Friedrich, Margrave of Baden-Durlach, seemed to fill the bill: he had literary interests and was a friend of Voltaire's. Boswell set himself to gain the star and ribbon of Karl Friedrich's Order of Fidelity, and when he was taking leave of the Margrave, with whom he had established friendly relations, actually asked for it. 'Let me have your genealogy attested, and when you return, we shall see,' said the Margrave; but nothing came of it.

Boswell was more successful in his next plan, which he pursued with passion: this was to be personally received by Rousseau, now, at fifty-two, living in seclusion at the small mountain village of Môtiers in the territory of Neuchâtel. He had got the Earl Marischal to give him a note simply presenting compliments to Rousseau (whom the Earl had protected when he was Governor of Neuchâtel) and seeking news of his health, but Boswell wanted a more direct approach. He wrote, with several revisions, a letter to Rousseau in which he presented himself as just the sort of person Rousseau would want to meet, having prepared himself by reading the *Nouvelle Héloïse* and *Emile*. Putting up at the inn at Môtiers, he sent the maid to Rousseau with the letter. Rousseau replied that though he was unwell and in no state to receive visitors he could not deny himself to Mr Boswell provided he would make his visit short. The letter had worked. Boswell obtained six interviews with Rousseau on five different days, and equally impressed both the great man and his mistress Thérèse Le Vasseur.

Rousseau conveying his mistress, Thérèse Le Vasseur (talking to the dog Sultan) and two friends to an island in the Lac de Bienne. Here he sought refuge from attacks by bigoted villagers.

Boswell was a genius in drawing people out and in using his own confidences to gain the interest and affection of the person interviewed. He timed each remark with precision, knew when to be humorous, when off-hand, when pressing, and when not to take 'no' for an answer. The interviews as he records them in his somewhat uncertain French are achievements of the utmost virtuosity. At the first interview Boswell prevailed by sheer determination; at the second he allowed Rousseau to do nearly all the talking; but at the third he embarked at once on the story of his own life. Rousseau sent him away after Boswell had asked him to 'assume direction' of him. 'I cannot,' replied Rousseau. 'I can be responsible only for myself.' He told Boswell he was in pain, and must be alone ('I need a chamber-pot every other minute': he had a painful constriction of the urethra). Boswell went, his story only partly told, but insisted he would be back.

To ease his return he wrote and sent Rousseau a long autobio-graphical account of himself. When he came back to Môtiers on 14 December he found that Rousseau had read the document, and would see him that afternoon for fifteen minutes. Twenty minutes, Boswell insisted. Rousseau laughed. Boswell duly returned at four in the afternoon and talked about questions of religion and morality. What was wrong, he asked, with having a number of girls? 'Cannot I follow Oriental usage?' (A question Boswell asked himself and others throughout his life. He also sometimes called it 'patriarchal' usage.) Rousseau was not encouraging. The talk moved to a variety of topics, Boswell always calling the shots, and in the end Thérèse asked Boswell to dine with them the next day. At dinner on 15 December they again discussed many subjects, including questions of rank and social equality. They parted with mutual promises of corresponding and mutual expressions of friendship. The whole thing was an extraordinary success for Boswell not only as celebrity-hunter but also as genuine seeker of friendship and guidance from men of genius, a role which he played sincerely since it fulfilled a deep need of his nature.

Two weeks later, with a letter of introduction from Zélide's friend Constant d'Hermenches, he visited the seventy-year-old Voltaire at Ferney, near Geneva. Here were no autobiographical effusions, but short, dry witty remarks from Voltaire, and then Boswell's departure before dinner. Returning to Geneva, Boswell meditated his further tactics: he decided to write to Voltaire's niece, Mme Denis, who kept house for him, to seek her influence in being invited to spend a night under Voltaire's roof. Surprisingly, the reply, in Voltaire's hand and in English, contained the invitation. On 27 December he returned to Ferney. After dinner (in which Voltaire did not participate) he manœuvred to get Voltaire alone and, with remarkable persistence, engaged him in a probing conversation about the real nature of his beliefs. Ignoring Voltaire's ironies and evasions, his ridicule and

Voltaire: a contemporary caricature.

47

dismissive humour, and ignoring even an incipient fainting fit on Voltaire's part, he pressed him on his conception of God. Boswell wrote up the whole conversation in a long letter to Temple. Voltaire 'expressed his desire to resemble the Author of Goodness by being good himself. His sentiments go no further. He does not inflame his mind with grand hopes of the immortality of the soul. . . . I was moved; I was sorry. . . . I called to him with emotion, "Are you sincere? Are you really sincere?" He answered, "Before God, I am."' Boswell spent two nights at Ferney. Before leaving, Boswell returned to the question of the immortality of the soul, trying in vain to get Voltaire to admit its probability. Voltaire professed his scepticism: he did not know what the soul was. 'I know not the cause. I cannot judge. I cannot be a juryman.' Voltaire agreed to correspond with him. It was an incredible achievement for a young man confronting the great sage of the Enlightenment.

Having secured his father's reluctant permission to travel for four months in Italy, which was later extended for another month to enable him to study adequately the antiquities of Rome, Boswell crossed the Alps by the Mount Cenis Pass (a 'horribly grand' prospect) and arrived at Turin on 7 January 1765. He was in Italy as a student and sightseer, genuinely eager to observe and make notes on the relics of ancient Rome and the works of the Italian Renaissance. Wherever he went he viewed and described paintings, buildings,

The arrival of a young traveller and his suite in the Piazza di Spagna, Rome. In some such state, though with less retinue, Boswell must have arrived in February 1765.

places with classical and Christian associations, quoting classical authors when relevant. But he also associated Italy with the prospect of amorous adventures, which duly materialized both of the low and the genteel variety. The Italian convention of the *cavaliere servente* made it perfectly plausible for him to have an intrigue with a married lady in society, and, aware of this, he pursued several, on one occasion at least with notable success, but he also spent a fair amount of money on prostitutes (duly listed in his account of expenses). He had a lively two weeks in Turin before proceeding to Rome with many stops on the way to examine antiquities and scenes of interest. One such stop was Parma, where, with an introduction from Rousseau, he made friends with the French scholar Alexandre Deleyre.

John Wilkes, whom Boswell met in Rome, and liked.

He got to Rome on 15 February, and there met John Wilkes, now in virtual exile after his expulsion from the House of Commons, having been found guilty of both seditious libel and obscene and blasphemous libel. This lively, wholly immoral, triumphantly womanizing sceptic intrigued and in some respects delighted Boswell, in spite of his firm repudiation of Wilkes's principles. Wilkes in turn found Boswell appealing. They did not see much of each other at Rome, for Wilkes was on the point of leaving for Naples, but when Boswell caught up with him in that city they had some extremely lively conversations, duly noted down by Boswell.

Boswell found Rome disappointing, and solaced himself by a resolve to have a girl a day, which he apparently did. On 25 February he left Rome for Naples, returning to Rome on 24 March to spend twelve weeks there in serious study both of Roman antiquities (under the guidance of the Scottish antiquary Colin Morison) and the Italian language (with an Italian tutor). Catholic Rome appealed to him as much as ancient Rome, though for very different reasons, and he attended Easter mass at St Peter's on 7 April ('most grave and pious, quite sure there must be some truth beyond skies'). He had himself presented to the Pope as 'Baron Boswell'. He went to Frascati to see the Cardinal Duke of York, Bonnie Prince Charlie's younger brother, officiate at a Whitsunday mass. He met and became good friends with Andrew Lumisden, the veteran Jacobite and secretary to the now old and ailing father of Prince Charlie, the Old Pretender, who had lived nearly all his life in exile at Rome. Lumisden was a knowledgeable antiquary and took Boswell on several expeditions. His notes record monuments, churches, villas, paintings and girls. ('Night, new girl. Swear no women for week.' He was always making such resolutions, but they generally lasted less than a week.) He commissioned from the Scots historical painter in Rome, Gavin Hamilton, a painting of 'Mary Queen of Scots resigning her Crown', which he really could not afford, and had his portrait painted in his scarlet and gold suit with green fur-trimmed cloak by another Scots painter in Rome, George Willison.

He left Rome on 14 June, now travelling with Lord Mountstuart, the twenty-one-year-old son of Lord Bute, and Mountstuart's 'governor' Lieutenant-Colonel James Edmonstone and his tutor, the Swiss student of Scandinavian antiquities Paul Henri Mallet. They travelled to Venice together, but Boswell and Mountstuart bickered continually on the journey and Boswell found Mallet rude, bad-tempered, and offensive to himself personally. In Venice Boswell met Giuseppe Baretti, Johnson's friend and translator. From Venice they went to Monigo, and while there Mountstuart was summoned home by his father. This put Boswell into a predicament, since he had asked Lord Auchinleck for an extension of his travels on the understanding that he would travel with Mountstuart, whose powerful family connections would surely influence Auchinleck in his favour. With Mountstuart gone, Boswell knew he would be called home too. But there was much more he still wanted to see. So he simply did not write to his father and pretended to assume that he had his approval. He went back to Parma and renewed his confiding friendship with Deleyre. Then he went to Florence, where he spent two weeks. Then, in search of more sensual pleasures than looking at pictures and buildings, he went to Siena where – pursuing a long-cherished plan to have an Italian high-born lady as his mistress – he was eventually accepted by Girolama Piccolomini, who was genuinely distressed when he left Siena after a stay of five weeks. He was now determined to go to Corsica, and, after visiting Lucca and Pisa, went to Leghorn to arrange passage there. He sailed for Corsica from Leghorn on 11 October 1765.

Siena, where Boswell stayed five weeks for pleasures more sensual than cultural.

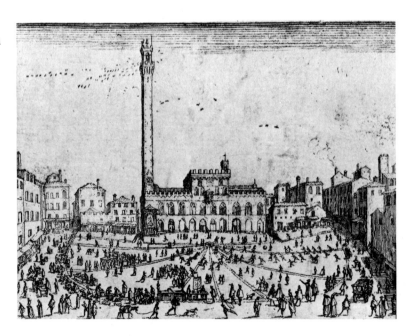

The portrait by George Willison
which Boswell commissioned in
Rome.

It was Rousseau who had stimulated in Boswell a lively interest in
Corsica and the Corsicans, that rugged people who had preserved
their national independence of feeling in spite of centuries of rule by a
long series of outsiders. It had long been ruled from the Republic of
Genoa, but both France and Britain became interested in Corsica
in the course of the continental wars of the eighteenth century. The
Corsicans, periodically asserting their independence against all
parties, fought against a French invasion of the island in 1738, under
Giacinto Paoli, who on his defeat and withdrawal into exile took
with him his son Pasquale. Pasquale Paoli returned to Corsica in

1755, with the title of 'General', as leader of the Corsicans in their fight for independence against both Genoese and French. He was a remarkable character, who had been educated in his exile at the Royal Academy of Naples and had studied the Greek and Roman classics – particularly the historians, Plutarch's *Lives* and Virgil – with passion. He had a high concept of himself as civilizer, improver and educator of Corsica as well as its military saviour. In the ten exciting years during which he ran Corsica he came to personify its character and ambitions and came near to giving viable form and practical reality to the island's long dream of independence. He became a legend in his own lifetime, and the kind of romantic legend that was bound to attract Boswell.

Landing at Centuri on the north-west tip of the island, Boswell moved south down the west coast to Nonza and then south again, through the interior, to Corte. There he found that Paoli was at Sollacarò, to the south-west across the mountains near Ajaccio, and he followed him there over extremely difficult mountain territory. Boswell had no special equipment for this arduous journey over rugged mountainous country: he travelled, with his servant, largely on foot, with his luggage carried on pack-animals ('sometimes horses, but oftener mules or asses') or on the heads of women, and he wore his normal elegant clothes. Evidence of the hardship involved were the ingrowing toenails he developed from walking down mountainsides: these gave him trouble for a long time afterwards. But in spite of difficulties and of most primitive conditions (eating chestnuts obtained by throwing stones at chestnut trees and drinking water from streams) Boswell found his journey over the mountains 'very entertaining'. 'I was in great health and spirits, and fully able to enter into the ideas of the brave rude men whom I found in all quarters.'

Boswell had letters of introduction to Paoli from Rousseau and from Count Antonio Rivarola, the Sardinian Consul at Leghorn, whom he had met there. When he was finally ushered into Paoli's presence at Sollacarò, the great man, whose physical presence met all Boswell's expectations, turned 'a steadfast, keen and penetrating eye' on him for some time, until Boswell was able to bring out his prepared introductory speech: he had been in Rome, he said. 'I am come from seeing the ruins of one brave and free people; I now see the rise of another.' Paoli later told Fanny Burney that at first he thought Boswell a spy, but soon discovered that he was wrong and that Boswell was 'a very good man'. Once rid of his suspicions, Paoli treated Boswell handsomely and the two got on excellently together. He put him up at a decayed but magnificent mansion and had him treated like a visiting ambassador. (Indeed, many of the locals called him 'the English ambassador' and Boswell was not averse to having people believe that that was his role and that he was in Corsica to promise British help for the Corsicans against the French.) The restrained but

Pasquale Paoli: 'a steadfast, keen and penetrating eye'.

heroic rhetoric of Paoli's conversation deeply impressed Boswell, who now felt that he had met and made friends with a true hero in the antique mode.

His Corsican enthusiasm grew daily. He had a Corsican outfit made for him, which he wore with Paoli's own pistols which the general presented to him. He entertained the Corsicans by playing on the flute (acquired and learned in Italy) and singing patriotic British songs. When Boswell left after ten days in Sollacarò, Paoli professed his friendship and Boswell 'took leave of Paoli with regret and agitation, not without some hopes of seeing him again'. Boswell wrote in triumph to John Johnston that, having made 'himself acquainted with one of the greatest Men in Europe, after having traversed the greatest part of this Island, and observed the free spirit of it's brave Inhabitants, I am very well satisfy'd with the singular tour which I have made.' His satisfaction had survived his journey back from Sollacarò to Corte in appalling weather which produced first a heavy cold and then malaria. He was looked after by the Franciscan fathers at Corte, but he had not fully recovered when he left Corte for Bastia, where he suffered a relapse and took twelve days to recover, attentively looked after by a French army physician provided by the Comte de Marbeuf, the French commander in Corsica, to whom Paoli had given him an introduction (the paradox of Paoli's being on excellent terms with the French commander is part of the complex pattern of chivalry with which Paoli conducted his relationships).

He set sail for Genoa on 20 November, but a storm forced the felucca to seek refuge at Capraia, 'a little rocky Island about six miles long' nearly twenty miles east of the northern tip of Corsica, and he

Woven badge worn by supporters of Paoli; this one was presented to Boswell.

53

stayed there, 'very comfortably lodged in a Franciscan Convent' though bored and irritated. The felucca finally sailed for Genoa on 30 November 1765. Among the letters Boswell found awaiting him at Genoa was one from his father saying that he had been seriously ill and expected his son to return quickly. Boswell realized it was time he set off for home. After some sightseeing and the usual note-making in Genoa, and some carefully calculated circulation of reports about his visit to Corsica and to Paoli and the political reverberations that could be expected – opening shots in his sustained battle to enlist British aid for Paoli and Corsican independence – he moved north via Marseilles, Avignon and Lyons to Paris. There, after attending a brothel on Saturday, 25 January and two church services (Roman Catholic and Church of England) on Sunday the 26th, he visited Wilkes, now living in Paris, and at his lodgings read in a copy of *The St. James's Chronicle* of the death of his mother. He could not take it in at first, and tried to push it from his mind by another visit to a brothel, but the next day a letter from his father confirmed the news and produced a mood of confused grief.

It was while he was in Paris that Boswell made his conditional offer of marriage to Zélide in a letter to her father, writing at the same time to his own father to ask if he could return home via Holland to propose in person. We have seen M. de Zuylen's reply; Lord Auchinleck's was even more discouraging and, knowing by now of his mother's death, Boswell had no option but to go straight home. He left Paris on 30 January, escorting Rousseau's mistress Thérèse Le Vasseur who was going to join Rousseau, now in England after having been invited by David Hume – at that time private secretary to the British Ambassador in Paris – to seek asylum there from his enemies on the Continent. While they were waiting for several days at an inn in Calais for the delayed departure of the Channel packet, Boswell seduced (or was seduced by) the forty-five-year-old Thérèse in circumstances that remain obscure, since Boswell's own account has been destroyed. He brought her to London and on 12 February he delivered her at Hume's London lodgings where Rousseau was staying. Boswell's feelings of respect and affection for Rousseau had been steadily ebbing away: he now thought him weak and sentimental, and sought him out no more. But he at once sought out Johnson, now living in Johnson's Court, Fleet Street, and was affectionately received. As his stay in London was brief, he could not see Johnson often, but even so the renewal of contact heightened his veneration for him and comparison of Johnson 'with many of the most celebrated persons of other countries' only 'increased and confirmed' his 'admiration of his extraordinary mind'. Johnson, who told Boswell he considered Rousseau 'a rascal who ought to be hunted out of society as he has been', did nothing to restore Boswell's admiration for the man he had so idolized a few months before.

In London Boswell carried on his campaign on behalf of Paoli and Corsica, and actually managed to get an interview with William Pitt – not at this time a member of the Government but still of enormous influence – but was able to get from him no more than an affirmation that 'I should be sorry that in any corner of the world, however distant or however small, it should be suspected that I could ever be indifferent to the cause of liberty.' Boswell planted paragraphs in newspapers about his Corsican visit and about the Corsican situation, not only to boost his own importance but also out of genuine zeal for Corsican independence. It was of course all good advance publicity for the account of Corsica and his travels there that he was now determined to write, but that book was itself planned as part of his political campaign. The campaign failed in its main object, to get British Government help for Paoli. When the French invaded Corsica in 1768, Boswell raised money and guns for Paoli, but to no avail: Corsican resistance was finally crushed at the Battle of Ponte Novo in May 1769, and Paoli preferred exile in England to surrendering to French rule. He spent the rest of his life in London, maintaining the most cordial relations with Boswell, whose admiration for the great man and pride in having him as a friend never diminished.

William Pitt, first Earl of Chatham. Boswell approached him on behalf of Paoli, and received sympathy but no commitment.

Boswell was back in Auchinleck in March, having stopped at Newcastle to see his brother John, whose mental illness now made it necessary for him to be confined there under the care of a dissenting clergyman. On his arrival home he was well received by his father, who offered to coach him personally for the Scots law examination he would have to take. Boswell himself was at first dispirited, but soon cheered himself up by falling in love with the gardener's daughter, Euphemia Bruce, and indulging in romantic fancies of marriage with a devoted social inferior who would live with him 'just as a mistress, without the disgrace and remorse'. But a visit to Moffat turned his mind away from Euphemia towards an attractive young woman there, Mrs Dodds, living separated from her husband and three children. She was equally attracted to Boswell and quickly became his mistress. Later Boswell brought her to Edinburgh and arranged lodgings for her there. She bore him a daughter, Sally, at the end of 1767. Sally appears to have died in infancy: shortly after her birth Boswell disengaged himself from Mrs Dodds, on whom he spent a fair amount of money and with whom his relations, though often passionate, were sometimes turbulent. 'She is ill-bred, quite a rompish girl,' he wrote to Temple. 'She debases my dignity. She has no refinement.' But she was 'admirably formed for amorous dalliance' and he found it hard to break away from her.

In July 1766 Boswell passed his examination in Scots law and then, having written the necessary Latin thesis – a traditional but not exacting requirement – and passed his oral public examination in that, he was formally admitted as a Scots advocate on 29 July. For the next seventeen years he practised law as an advocate in Edinburgh. It is important to remember that the Edinburgh law courts were the scene of Boswell's regular professional activity during the central and most important period in his life. He had other ambitions too, literary and political, and unfortunately he never realized how chimerical and how unsuited to his talents were the latter, pursuit of which virtually destroyed him in his last years. Nor did he ever realize how paramount was his genius as a biographer and diarist.

'I shall be attached to the generous woman for ever,' wrote Boswell to Temple of Mrs Dodds in May 1766, but at the same time he declared that this would be his 'last irregular connection' and that he was seriously thinking, as he had been off and on for some time, of marriage. He had met in London Elizabeth Bosville, daughter of a Yorkshire gentleman whom Boswell regarded, with doubtful probability, as the senior representative of his family (Bosville and Boswell, as well as other forms, derive from the Norman French Boisville, the family having originally come from Normandy after the Conquest), and for a while thought of her as a possible wife. Zélide was now definitely ruled out.

Thoughts of Miss Bosville faded when he met Catherine Blair, heiress of the Ayrshire estate of Adamton and a distant relative. Her social desirability led Boswell to persuade himself that he was romantically in love with her, though this did not keep him from casual adventures with prostitutes while he was courting her. Once, having got drunk drinking Miss Blair's health, he 'went to a bawdy house, and passed a whole night in the arms of a whore'. She was, he recorded, 'a whore worthy of Boswell if Boswell must have a whore'. Miss Blair was a candid and intelligent young lady, 'handsome, stately' and of 'good countenance' and accepted Boswell's friendship without any illusions about love. When he proposed to her in February 1768, after a constantly shifting relationship on his side and repeated rumours of her engagement first to one other gentleman and then to yet another, she told him frankly that he had no chance, though they would remain friends. 'Now that all is over, I see many faults in her which I did not see before,' he wrote Temple and appears to have been really rather relieved: he composed a comic song on the subject of his rejection, endeavouring 'to make merry on my misfortune'.

Congratulating himself on his escape from 'the insensible Miss Blair and the furious Zélide' he next whipped himself into a passion for a sixteen-year-old Irish girl, Mary Ann Boyd. *La belle irlandaise*, he called her, 'formed like a Grecian nymph with the sweetest countenance, full of sensibility, accomplished, with a Dublin education, . . . her father a counsellor-at-law with an estate of £1,000 a year and above £10,000 in ready money'. He followed her to Ireland in the spring of 1769, taking with him his cousin Margaret

Margaret Montgomerie, Boswell's cousin and – after his many rebounds – his wife.

Montgomerie, with whom he had long been on terms of close friendship. But in his heart he knew that, for all his romantic gestures, his love for Miss Boyd was desperately *voulu* and in his cousin's company his will to keep this up steadily declined. The fact is he had long known subconsciously that his cousin was the woman for him. Two years older than Boswell, not strikingly beautiful, but intelligent, determined, patient and far from unattractive, she had been the recipient of Boswell's confidences for years. She loved him, and she wanted him as a husband, and in the end Boswell's constantly seeking her advice and even help in his marriage projects ended in his decision to marry her. He returned from Ireland without *la belle irlandaise* and in Edinburgh on 20 July 1769 wrote to his cousin formally proposing marriage and asking whether, if his father disapproved, she would be willing to share her life with him in exile on the Continent with his meagre prospect of £100 a year 'and the interest of your £1,000' (she was no heiress). She agreed, but this drastic step proved unnecessary, since Lord Auchinleck agreed to the marriage, although with reluctance. Margaret was the orphaned daughter of Lord Auchinleck's sister and lived with her married older sister at the family estate of Lainshaw, some seventeen miles north-west of Auchinleck. It was at Lainshaw that she and Boswell were married on 25 November 1769.

But this is to look ahead. In the summer of 1766 Boswell was at work on his book on Corsica, collecting such materials as he could and consulting everybody he could locate who had knowledge of the island. He also continued to plant stories in newspapers calculated to enlist interest in and sympathy for the Corsicans. Sir David Dalrymple (now a Lord of Session and styled Lord Hailes) encouraged him, and advised him to cut down on the historical part and concentrate on Paoli. Johnson wrote in August approving Boswell's resolution to obey his father, encouraging him to pursue the law 'vigorously and constantly', and telling him to forget about Corsica. 'Mind your own affairs, and leave the Corsicans to others.' But Boswell earnestly defended his zeal for Corsica, and continued to prepare his book. He wrote to Pitt in September and again in January seeking his influence on behalf of Corsica and Paoli.

Meanwhile he was active in the law, attending the circuits of the Judiciary Court, in the hope of being appointed by the court to defend poor clients, which was a regular way of beginning a career as advocate. In Glasgow in September 1766 Boswell obtained his first criminal client, one John Reid, a rough character with a bad reputation, who was accused of stealing one hundred and twenty sheep from a Peeblesshire farm and driving them to Glasgow to sell to the butchers. The charge was capital in the eighteenth century, and Boswell threw himself with zeal into the defence. Reid had certainly offered the stolen sheep for sale, and, as he admitted to Boswell, he had stolen sheep before; but on this occasion he insisted that he had accepted the sheep in good faith from another man who had commissioned him to sell them in Glasgow. Boswell believed him and allowed himself to become emotionally involved in proving his innocence. He visited Reid in the Tolbooth prison in Edinburgh and provided food as well as religious consolation. In the end Boswell and his fellow advocate Andrew Crosbie who assisted him on the case were able to get the jury to return the Scots verdict of 'not proven'. The judges of the Justiciary Court (one of whom was Lord Auchinleck) thought that the jury had found against the evidence, and said so. This was to prove important, for when Reid was again accused of sheep-stealing in the summer of 1774 and Boswell again defended him, the judges remembered what they considered his real guilt at the previous trial and spoke of Reid to the jury in highly prejudicial terms, which proved a factor in Reid's being found guilty and hanged. This, as we

shall see, proved a traumatic experience for Boswell, for on this
occasion too he threw himself into the defence with a kind of morbid
personal anxiety. This passionate personal involvement in his clients,
already displaying itself in Boswell's first criminal case, aroused the
distrust of the legal authorities in Edinburgh and was probably a
factor in preventing him from rising to the top of the profession.
Henry Dundas, a year and a half his junior, whom Boswell and
Temple had patronized when all three were students at Edinburgh,
was appointed Solicitor-General before Boswell had even 'passed
advocate' and was to rise to the commanding heights both legal and
political to become 'King Harry the Ninth' and virtual ruler of
Scotland. 'Do you remember what you and I used to think of Dundas?'
Boswell wrote to Temple on hearing of his appointment as Solicitor-
General: for the rest of his life he was to be jealous and resentful. A
political career like Dundas's was simply beyond Boswell's reach.

Boswell continued to introspect on his own character. 'I am a
singular man,' he wrote in a notebook entitled Memorabilia',
probably in 1767. 'I have the whim of an Englishman to make me think
and act extravagantly, and yet I have the coolness and good sense of a
Scotsman to make me sensible of it.' He concluded this self-description
by noting: 'I am a weaker man than can well be imagined. My
brilliant qualities are like embroidery upon gauze.' What Boswell is
diagnosing here is less a mixture of English and Scottish qualities

Henry Dundas, first Viscount
Melville.

than a characteristic of the Scottish character itself, what Gregory
Smith called (and the poet Hugh MacDiarmid delightedly repeated)
the 'Caledonian Antisyzygy', the tendency, recurring in Scottish
literature, to yoke together opposite extremes, 'the sudden jostling of
contraries'. On 9 May 1767 Boswell noted down two alternative
views of the family hypochondria: either the family were 'all crack-
brained' or they were 'remarkable for genius and worth' but afflicted
with a cast of melancholy 'often the attendant of distinguished minds'.

The other dominant concern of Boswell at this time was the Douglas
cause, the most important civil trial in eighteenth-century Scotland.
Archibald, Duke of Douglas, had died without direct heirs in 1761;
his sister, Lady Jane Douglas, had in 1746 at the age of forty-eight
married Colonel John Stewart and in 1748 in Paris announced the
birth of twins, of whom one died young. The circumstances of the
birth were highly obscure, and the likelihood of a fifty-year-old
woman bearing children far from strong. The surviving child,
Archibald Douglas (he had assumed the Douglas surname in 1761),
if really the son of Lady Jane Douglas, was the true heir of the Douglas
estates. If he was not the true son of Lady Jane, then the estates went to
the Duke of Hamilton (or conceivably to another relative). Lawyers
acting for the guardians of Hamilton and his brother alleged that the
children claimed to be the sons of Lady Jane Douglas were in fact
abducted French children and produced a very damaging case indeed
against the Douglas claim. Lady Jane had died in 1753 and her husband, having seen Archibald take possession of the Douglas estates,
was also by now dead. Everything depended on the evidence of surviv-

ing witnesses or authentic documents, but the alleged witness of the birth of the twins could not be found, the testimony of Lady Jane's companion Helen Hewit that she had been present at the birth was highly suspect, and four letters in French purporting to have been written by the French surgeon who delivered the babies were patently botched up later by someone (most plausibly John Stewart himself) whose native language was English. Nobody who looks at the evidence today can avoid the very strong suspicion that the Douglas case was based on fraud by the alleged parents.

Boswell, however, thought otherwise. He believed passionately in what he called 'that great principle of law – *filiation* – on which we all depend' and thought that if the parents' account of their children's birth were discredited family stability and the prospect of assured inheritance were threatened (it will be remembered that his father had at one time threatened to disinherit Boswell himself). So Boswell threw himself with passionate partisanship into defence of the Douglas cause and attack on the Hamilton party. While the case was being argued in the Court of Session early in 1767 he composed a song attacking the Hamiltonians, and the following May composed a companion song championing the Douglasites. On 15 June Boswell published a curious prose romance entitled *Dorando* with the main characters allegorical presentations of Archibald Douglas (the Prince of Dorando) and the young Duke of Hamilton (the Prince of Arvidoso): it caused something of a sensation and produced a prosecution of the publishers, which failed of serious consequences largely as a result of Boswell's mocking anonymous articles on the subject in the press. In July the Court of Session found against Douglas, but the Douglas lawyers appealed to the House of Lords which reversed this decision in February 1769, thus leaving Archibald Douglas in possession of the Douglas estates. Boswell continued to give his unofficial aid to Douglas so long as the final decision was in doubt. In November 1767 he published a lucid and succinct account of the case in favour of Douglas, reduced from four thousand pages of legal documents, and in the same month there appeared his *Letters of Lady Jane Douglas*, a tendentious selection of that lady's private correspondence. When Douglas was vindicated in the House of Lords appeal Boswell led an Edinburgh mob in wild celebration of the victory: the mob insisted on prominent citizens illuminating their houses for the victory and broke the windows of judges (including Boswell's own father) when they refused to do so. Douglas showed less gratitude for all this than Boswell expected. He retained him as a regular counsel after the victory was won, but deprecated Boswell's constant harking back to the legal conflict and finally broke with him after Boswell had reported in his *Journal of a Tour to the Hebrides* that Johnson had supported the Hamilton side and had roundly asserted that Lady Jane Douglas was *not* Archibald Douglas's mother.

Archibald Douglas, central figure in the 'Douglas cause'.

An Account of Corsica, the Journal of a Tour to That Island; and Memoirs of Pascal Paoli, by James Boswell, Esq., was published in February 1768, and made a great impression, running to three editions in England, three in Ireland, and many translations. But it had no effect on British Government policy. The liveliest part of the book is not the introductory geographical and historical account, derived from secondary sources, but his own vivid account of his journey and his conversations with Paoli. Johnson himself had to praise the book. 'Your history is like other histories, but your Journal is in a very high degree curious and delightful . . . I know not whether I could name any narrative by which curiosity is better excited or better gratified.' Henceforth Boswell was 'Corsica Boswell', identified in the public mind with an enthusiasm for the cause of Corsican independence.

Boswell went to London again after the Court of Session had risen in the spring of 1768, setting out on 16 March and leaving for the north again on 9 June in order to be in Edinburgh for the Court's summer term. He travelled by chaise, not this time as an unknown young Scot seeking preferment in London but as a known author coming to receive merited recognition. *En route* he visited and admired York Minster and engaged strangers in conversation about Corsica (to be gratified on discovering that his book was known). He felt completely self-assured. Formerly, he wrote in his Journal, his mind had been a lodging-house for all sorts of ideas, whereas now it was a house where, though strangers were welcome on the 'street rooms and upper floors . . . yet there is always a settled family in the back parlour and sleeping-closet behind it'. He arrived in London on 22 March, his arrival heralded in the newspapers in accounts which he had contributed himself. He got good lodgings in Half Moon Street and a Somersetshire lad for a servant, and went off to see an execution at Tyburn, observing the conduct of the victim in the greatest detail. Then he went to Mr Dilly, the bookseller who had published his book. Wilkes was now back, standing for Parliament amid a frenzied 'Wilkes and Liberty' roaring by the mob, and Boswell noted it all, though he stayed away from Wilkes personally as not being a proper associate for a rising advocate and author with his own political ambitions. Johnson was not in London, he found, but on a visit to Oxford, where Boswell followed him and spent three days listening to and recording the high points of his conversation. Johnson was as affectionate as ever. When Boswell told him he had made £200 by the law that year, Johnson 'grumbled and laughed and was wonderfully pleased. What, Bozzy? Two hundred pounds! A great deal.'

Back in London Boswell picked up a 'red-haired hussy' and wallowed 'in the very sink of vice'. He called on, and was called on by, large numbers of distinguished people. For a while he was confined to his room with a venereal infection. All the time he continued his propaganda for Corsica. Johnson returned from Oxford in May,

and they supped and talked together as before. It was a full, diverse, contradictory and characteristically Boswellian life he led before returning to Edinburgh in June. There for a while, letting his Journal lapse, he disappears from sight into his legal work. In December there appeared a collection of *British Essays in Favour of the Brave Corsicans*, edited by Boswell, seven of the twenty essays being by Boswell himself, the rest taken from newspapers. Their arguments in favour of Britain's taking Corsica under her wing were of no avail.

In July 1769, just when Boswell was working himself up to propose to his cousin, he was astounded and horrified to learn from his father that he contemplated remarrying. The prospect drove him to absolute fury. He threatened to break with his father altogether and retire abroad, and wrote an extraordinary essay, *On Second Marriages: A True Story in Queen Anne's Reign*, in which a son, horrified at his father's determination to marry again, 'retired to a distant country' while the father, soon perceiving that 'age and distemper are miserably suited for conjugal society', sank into 'folly and dotage' to die finally 'in great agony both of body and mind', thus providing a lesson in 'decorum and generosity of conduct to those who come after him'.

John Wilkes ('Wilkes and Liberty') before the Court of King's Bench in 1768. Boswell had enjoyed his company in Naples, but a rising advocate with political ambitions could no longer associate with a loose-living radical.

David Hume, the philosopher. Boswell found his blend of virtue and scepticism disturbing.

It is difficult to find a rational explanation of Boswell's hysterical response to his father's plan. Lord Auchinleck was sixty-two, his proposed wife, Elizabeth Boswell, forty or a little older. Did he feel that his father might produce another son to whom he would leave the estate? He certainly felt that his father's plan was shockingly offensive to him personally as well as somehow monstrously obscene. His friends tried to soothe him. When he told his mother's uncle, Basil Cochrane, Commissioner of Customs, of his father's proposal, the Commissioner expressed astonishment but would not accept Boswell's violent views. 'No,' he said, 'you must make the best of it.' And that is what he had to do. His father and Elizabeth Boswell, who was the daughter of John Boswell of Balmuto and a cousin of Lord Auchinleck, were married on the same day that Boswell married *his* cousin.

At the time of his acceptance by Margaret Boswell was busy with legal work. 'I have cleared twenty guineas,' he noted of his week's work on 29 July. 'My dearest Margaret is my great object,' he added. He seemed surprised at his own ability to lead simultaneously a busy professional life and a gay social life in the absence of his fiancée. He noted in his Journal that it was impossible to record adequately his inner mental and emotional variations. 'I defy any man to write down anything like a perfect account of what he has been conscious during one day of his life, if in any degree of spirits. But he will do what he can.' David Hume called to give his 'philosophical opinion' that the marriage would be happy. The kindheartedness and general virtuous-ness of this sceptical philosopher puzzled and deeply disturbed Boswell. 'Were it not for his infidel writings everybody would love him.' That a thoughtful and virtuous man could get along admirably in life without accepting Christianity or believing in a 'future state' was a threat to everything Boswell wanted to believe. Years later, when Hume was dying in July 1776, Boswell called on and interviewed the dying man in the desperate hope of finding his scepticism collapse, but instead he found the philosopher facing death and the prospect of annihilation with complete equanimity. Boswell, who was constantly seeking reassurance about the truth of Christianity and the reality of immortality (something that he got regularly from Dr Johnson), was haunted by this scene for years. He tried to persuade himself that Hume must have been secretly a believer, and at last on 8 January 1784, having had an 'agreeable dream' that he found a diary kept by Hume in which he had recorded that in spite of his published defences of scepticism and infidelity 'he was in reality a Christian and a very pious Man', he was able to get the matter out of his system.

Boswell set out for London again on 28 August 1769, after the rising of the Court of Session. It was strange that a recently engaged man should have been so eager to leave his fiancée. He told himself

Dr Johnson: portrait by Sir Joshua
Reynolds. The Great Cham was the
last of Boswell's father-figures.

and others that he needed medical treatment in London for the purifica-
tion of his blood, but it seems that he really wanted to see Johnson and
have a last fling in the metropolis. The more Boswell quarrelled with
his father the more Johnson emerged as his true father-figure, what
Stephen Dedalus in *Ulysses* would have called his 'transubstantial'
father who would replace his unsatisfactory 'consubstantial' father.
This time he stayed with Charles Dilly in London and not in lodgings.
On calling at Johnson's Court he was disappointed to find that
Johnson was staying in Brighton with his friends Mr and Mrs Thrale.
Mr Thrale was a wealthy brewer and his wife was a lady of literary
pretensions who was a devoted admirer of Johnson and a collector of
his sayings. She and Boswell soon recognized each other as rival
Johnsonians and in later life the rivalry led to real enmity. Johnson
spent long periods with the Thrales in their splendid villa at Streatham,
where Boswell was also to be a guest, but never an intimate as Johnson
became.

Boswell had hoped that Johnson would go with him to Stratford to the great Shakespeare Jubilee planned by David Garrick (the beginning of the Shakespeare industry at Stratford), but Johnson was not interested. Boswell – who had originally decided not to go but to stay in London and receive medical treatment – eventually decided to go alone and to attend the festivities in the costume of a Corsican chief, which he had to get specially made since he had left his genuine Corsican costume at Edinburgh. He arrived in Stratford on 6 September, the day the three-day festival began. In spite of almost continuous rain the ceremonies went off as planned – first, the firing of a cannon at dawn, then parades, masquerade balls, firework displays and the recitation by Garrick in a specially built amphitheatre of his specially composed *Ode upon Dedicating a Building, and Erecting a Statue, to Shakespeare.* Boswell shamelessly used the proceedings as a platform both for Corsica and for his own ego. On the second day of the celebrations he composed and actually arranged to have immediately printed a set of verses 'in the Character of a Corsican at Shakespeare's Jubilee' for distribution to the public. At the masquerade his attendance as a Corsican chief created something of a sensation. 'My Corsican dress attracted everybody,' he noted. 'I was as much a favourite as I could desire.' He wrote an account of his appearance for a number of periodicals. 'One of the most remarkable masks upon this occasion', said *The London Magazine* (i.e. Boswell, anonymously), 'was James Boswell, Esq., in the dress of an armed Corsican chief. . . . He wore a short dark-coloured coat of coarse cloth, scarlet waistcoat and breeches, and black spatterdashes. His cap or bonnet was of black cloth; on the front of it was embroidered in gold letters VIVA LA LIBERTÀ, and on one side of it was a handsome blue feather and cockade.' The Stratford junketings were on the whole considered a failure, but Boswell was infinitely satisfied with his own costumed prancings and considered his three days at Stratford well spent.

Back in London, Boswell wrote to Johnson and to Mrs Thrale ('I told you, madam, that you and I were rivals for that great man') with news of his proposed marriage; he said that if Johnson could not come back to London he, Boswell, would wait upon him at Brighton. But Johnson did come back to London, after which, as Boswell tells us in the *Life*, 'we met frequently, and I continued the practice of making notes of his conversations, though not with so much assiduity as I wish I had done.' In the course of their various conversations Johnson said that 'a woman would not be the worse wife for being learned', a view which Boswell could not accept; for him, women were not to compete with men intellectually, and the most one wanted was that they should be 'sensible and well informed'.

Boswell fulfilled his ostensible purpose in coming to London by putting himself under the care of the aged Dr Kennedy, who, though 'a gaping babbler', had invented a decoction believed to cure 'every

J. Wale del.   J. Miller Sc.

JAMES BOSWELL Esq.ʳ

In the Dress of an Armed Corsican Chief, as he appear'd at
Shakespeare's Jubilee, at Stratford upon Avon September 1769.

'Corsica Boswell'.

The Thrales' house in Streatham.

species of scurvy, even to that of leprosy'. This, Kennedy's Diet Drink, was prescribed for Boswell, which made him 'very easy'. He now moved from Dilly's to lodgings in Carey Street, to be nearer Kennedy. Immediately afterwards he discovered that Paoli had arrived in London and had been lodged in magnificent apartments (at the expense of the British Government, which would not save Corsican independence but which would happily provide for Paoli in exile in England) in Old Bond Street. When Paoli learned who his visitor was, even though he was still in his 'night-gown and night-cap' he gave a shout, then 'ran to me, took me all in his arms, and held me there for some time'. Boswell then moved from Carey Street to rooms in Old Bond Street, to be near Paoli, whom he went on to see frequently and to whom he confided all his personal problems about his relations with his father and his forthcoming marriage. For a while, Paoli almost replaced Johnson as a father-figure. But he continued to see a great deal of Johnson also, keeping at him with probing questions ('If, Sir, you were shut up in a castle, and a new-born child with you, what would you do?') and recording the answers even when they produced not a reply but an outburst, such as that which he received when he pressed his favourite subject of death ('Give us no more of this'). Boswell managed to bring Johnson and Paoli together, with gratifying results. Johnson 'said General Paoli had the loftiest port of any man he had ever seen'. He also, as during his previous London visit, met regularly with his distinguished friends, to whom he now

Hester Thrale. She and Boswell were rivals in their attachment to Dr Johnson.

added Sir Joshua Reynolds. He wrote regularly to Margaret Montgomerie. He was invited to spend the night before his departure for the north at the Thrales in Streatham, with Johnson, which he did. The next day, 11 November, Johnson accompanied him to London and saw him into the post-chaise that was to carry him to Scotland. On 25 November Margaret added her signature at Lainshaw to the marriage contract between herself and Boswell which Boswell had already had witnessed in London on 31 October by his two father-figures, Johnson and Paoli. On 5 December the newly married couple moved into a house of their own in the Cowgate, Edinburgh. The following May they moved to more spacious apartments in Chessel's Land, in the Canongate.

Marriage was good for Boswell. His wife (his 'valuable friend' as he so often called her in his Journal) was loyal, devoted and understanding, though eventually she had to reconcile herself as best she could to the fact that Boswell was more highly sexed than she and was periodically tempted, especially after drinking, to sordid adventures with prostitutes. But he genuinely loved her and she remained a stabilizing influence on him all her life. Things went very well in the early months. Boswell was kept busy with his professional legal work; he relished himself in his role as loving husband; he stayed sober. In June 1770 he wrote to Temple that he was now 'on very good terms' with his father. In August their first child, a son, died soon after birth, which distressed him, but not excessively or for very long for the experience of losing an infant was common enough at that time. In the winter of 1770–71 the Boswells moved again, this time to a flat in James's Court in the Lawnmarket which David Hume had formerly occupied: Boswell found it 'large enough for us, very convenient, and exceedingly healthful and pleasant'. In the autumn of 1771 he spent some time at Auchinleck studying Scots law and estate management with his father; Margaret, who had accompanied him on a similar visit to Auchinleck in October 1770, did not come this time, and Boswell suffered in her absence. To Boswell's delight, Paoli visited Scotland in the summer of 1771 and Boswell showed him round Edinburgh and took him on a tour of the West of Scotland from Auchinleck to Loch Lomond. He quarrelled with Lord Hailes as a result of an anonymous newspaper attack (by Boswell) on the Lord Provost of Edinburgh for failing to confer the freedom of the city on Paoli. He defended one George Macdonald against charges of stealing an ox and seventeen sheep, getting him acquitted on the former but not the latter charge, with a sentence, however, not of death but of transportation. On 3 March 1772 he wrote to Johnson saying he was coming to London to arrange their voyage to the Hebrides. He was also to appear in an appeal from the Court of Session to the House of Lords on behalf of a schoolmaster who had

High Street, Edinburgh, as it looked when Boswell showed Paoli the city.

been dismissed for excessive severity in physical chastisement of his pupils. The prospect of a London visit prompted him to resume his Journal, after a gap since shortly before his marriage.

He was in London from 19 March until 8 May 1772. After a little trouble he found good lodgings in Conduit Street and set out calling on friends and acquaintances. He had already visited Paoli, and saw much of him during his stay. 'My views in coming to London this spring were: to refresh my mind in the variety and spirit of the metro-polis, the conversation of my revered friend Mr. Samuel Johnson and that of other men of genius and learning; to try if I could to get something for myself, or be of service to any of my friends by means of the Duke of Queensberry, Lord Mountstuart, or Douglas; to be employed in Scotch appeals in the house of Lords, and also to see how the land might lie for me at the English bar; . . .' In the first of these objectives alone was he completely successful. Boswell's London Journal for the spring of 1772 records numerous conversations with Johnson which he was to use, often verbatim, in the *Life*. The immediacy of his pictures of Johnson (and of Garrick and Goldsmith and others) is sometimes startling. We see them frankly as they impinged on Boswell, who remains the centre of the stage. In the foreground always is Boswell's nervous egotism, his passionate concern with the state of his own mind and heart, his compulsive combination of hero-worship and exhibitionism. His excitement at being in London led him to think more and more of coming to the English Bar. 'My only objection is that I have a kind of idea of Scottish patriotism that makes me think it a duty to spend money in my own country . . . I am, however, resolved to go through the form of being called to the English bar.' Much though he missed his wife, there were moments in London when he felt himself at the height of human felicity. 'The place of our meeting, St. Paul's Churchyard, the sound of St. Paul's clock striking the hours, the busy and bustling coun-tenances of the partners around me, all contributed to give me a complete sensation of the kind [that he was a man of consequence]. I hugged myself in it.' Or again, dining at General Oglethorpe's house in the company of Johnson and Goldsmith: 'I just sat and hugged myself in my own mind. Here I am in London, at the house of General Oglethorpe, who introduced himself to me just because I had distinguished myself [over Corsica]; and here is Mr. Johnson, whose character is so vast; here is Dr. Goldsmith, so distinguished in literature. Words cannot describe our feelings. The finer parts are lost, as the down upon a plum; the radiance of light cannot be painted.' He spoke well in the House of Lords on behalf of the Scottish school-master, and though he lost the appeal was happy with his performance. He left London by the west road (Loughborough, Manchester, Shap, Carlisle, Langholm and Hawick) on 12 May, and was home on the 16th.

'Here is Dr Goldsmith, so distinguished in literature.'

Letter from Johnson to Goldsmith, proposing Boswell for membership of The Club.

Back in Edinburgh he was kept busy with his legal work, produced a certain amount of journalism, participated in Masonic activities, corresponded with his London friends, developed a passion for late-night gambling at cards, and occasionally, with his wife pregnant again, showed restiveness under the restraints of monogamy and once at least, after drinking, resorted to a prostitute. (He always confessed these matters to his wife, who reproved him, forgave him and advised him.) His daughter Veronica, to whom he became devoted, was born in March 1773 when Boswell was heavily involved in a number of criminal trials. He proudly announced his daughter's birth in letters to his friends. His wife safely delivered, and the Court having risen, Boswell lost little time in making what he now considered his annual spring visit to London. He set out on 30 March and was in London for six weeks. He got rooms in Piccadilly, to be near Paoli whom he visited immediately on arrival. His second visit was to Johnson. He saw both men frequently during his stay, and continued his recording of Johnson's conversation. On 30 April he was elected a

Boswell, Goldsmith and Johnson (left to right) at the Mitre Tavern in Fleet Street.

member of the famous Club (also known as the Literary Club) which included among its original members Johnson, Reynolds, Burke and Goldsmith; he was delighted to be 'introduced to such a society as can seldom be found'. His old friend Temple, now rector of the small parish of Mamhead, Devonshire, came to London with his wife to see him, and set out with him on 11 May on his journey north. Temple stayed a week (without his wife) with Boswell in Edinburgh.

Summer 1773 was a busy time, with cases before the General Assembly as well as the Court of Session. In July he won an important case for the Edinburgh bookseller Alexander Donaldson which established the right to publish books not expressly protected by the Copyright Act. He also had two criminal cases: he unsuccessfully defended Thomas Gray, a poor man who mistakenly stabbed his best friend when rushing out of the house after being intolerably baited by a group of youngsters, and two tinkers who had robbed and attacked (with fatal effect) a family in a lonely moorland cottage.

The great tour begins with a fond embrace as Johnson steps out of his post-chaise in the Canongate.

He was also busy arranging for Johnson's visit to Scotland, something on which he had set his heart. Johnson arrived in Edinburgh on 14 August, three days after the rising of the Court of Session, so that Boswell was free to look after him, and the great tour began.

It is not difficult to see why Johnson allowed himself to be persuaded to visit Scotland and in particular the Western Isles. Although he was notorious for his anti-Scottish prejudice, Johnson, like many other Englishmen and Lowland Scots of his time, was intensely curious to see for himself how a people considered to be living in an ancient form of society long extinct elsewhere in Britain actually conducted themselves. The Highlanders and Islanders were regarded as primitives, of the highest sociological interest, who lived on the brink of yet outside civilization, speaking a crude and ancient language. The sixty-four-year-old English sage thus came to Scotland to increase his knowledge and understanding of human society. It was a tough

Johnson, shown the sights (and scents) of Edinburgh, grumbles in Bozzie's ear, 'I smell you in the dark!'

and adventurous journey none the less, especially for a man of his age, involving as it did journeys over the most rugged country by foot or on horseback and sea passages in small boats in stormy weather. He would never have undertaken it if Boswell had not kept persuading him and enlisted the help of Scottish *literati* to second his requests. Boswell, as might have been expected, kept notes of the journey and of reactions to and by Johnson, and published them in his *Journal of a Tour to the Hebrides with Samuel Johnson* in 1785, after Johnson's death and more than ten years after the appearance of Johnson's own account, *A Journey to the Western Islands of Scotland*. Johnson's account is informative to the point of pedantry, sententious and, it must be admitted, rather dull. Boswell's is vivid, lively, full of colourful details, and of course constantly enlivened with the great man's conversation.

Johnson's post-chaise arrived at Boyd's Inn at the head of the Canongate in the evening, and there Boswell met him and conducted him along the High Street to his house in James's Court. This Court was one of the most elegant in the Old Town – the New Town was now being built but that was not Boswell's Edinburgh – and though Johnson was impressed with it he was good-humouredly disgusted at the insanitary state of Edinburgh's famous High Street. The contents of chamber-pots were discharged each evening from the windows of the tall flats, to accompanying shouts of 'gardyloo' ('gardez l'eau').

As Boswell and Johnson walked arm-in-arm in the dusk up the High Street, both were conscious of 'the evening effluvia of Edinburgh'. 'As we marched slowly along, he grumbled in my ear, "I smell you in the dark!" ' This is the first Johnsonian anecdote in the *Journal*, and one of the best known, since it is illustrated in a well-known engraving by Thomas Rowlandson.

Members of the Edinburgh *literati* came to pay tribute to Johnson during his three days at Edinburgh. Mrs Boswell gave up her own bed-chamber to the Sage, as Boswell gratefully recorded, and took a worse. On 18 August Johnson and Boswell, and a Bohemian servant called Joseph Ritter, set out from Edinburgh. They crossed the Forth,

Portree on the Isle of Skye.

and took a post-chaise from Kinghorn to St Andrews, where they saw the sights and the professors. Then on to Aberdeen, with a stop at Lord Monboddo's 'poor old house' and lively talk with the eccentric law lord. More sights and professors at Aberdeen. Then westward to Banff, where they got a fresh chaise, Cullen, Elgin (where they saw 'the noble ruins of the cathedral'), Forres, Fort George, to Inverness. From Inverness they went on horseback, proceeding along the southern shore of Loch Ness and through Glen Moriston and Glen Shiel to Glenelg, whence they got into a boat for Skye, landing at Armadale, to be received there by Sir Alexander Macdonald, who put them up at his house but did not, according to Boswell, entertain them very elegantly. On 6 September they went north on horseback by the shore to the farmhouse of Coirechatachan, where they were well entertained by 'Mr. Mackinnon'. Then they crossed over to Raasay in the Laird of Raasay's own boat, and there they were even more hospitably entertained. On 12 September they crossed back to Portree, where they stayed at an inn. They went on by horseback to Kingsburgh where they stayed with Allan Macdonald and were thrilled to meet his wife, the legendary Flora Macdonald. They reached Dunvegan Castle on the 13th, where they were happily entertained by the MacLeods and were agreeably confined by bad weather until the 19th.

Johnson and Boswell on their visit to Flora Macdonald. Prince Charles Edward's portrait hangs on the wall, a memento of the great days of the '45, twenty-eight years before.

Rowlandson's ribald comments on Boswell's *Journal of a Tour to the Hebrides* begin with the great man taking tea with his host and hostess. 'His address to her was most courteous and engaging, and his conversation soon charmed her into a forgetfulness of his external appearance.'

'We set out from Edinburgh, attended only by my man Joseph Ritter, a Bohemian.'

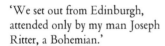

Stormy weather among the Hebrides. Donald Maclean of Coll 'put into my hand a rope which was fixed to the top of one of the masts, and told me to hold it till he bid me pull . . . his object was to keep me out of the way of those who were busy working the vessel.'

'After supper, we made a *procession* to *Saint Leonard's College* [St Andrews], the landlord walking before us with a candle, and the waiter with a lantern.'

'Though we had passed over not less than four-and-twenty miles of very rugged ground, and had a Highland dance on the top of *Dun Can* [on the island of Raasay, on 10 September 1773] . . . we returned in the evening not at all fatigued.' Boswell's dancing companions were Malcolm MacLeod and 'two other gentlemen'.

'What, drunk yet?'

It was at Dunvegan that Johnson read as much of Boswell's journal of the tour as he had yet written and said, 'I take a great delight in reading it.' Their next stop was Ullinish, where they stayed with Alexander MacLeod, and then went on to Talisker. Then they crossed the island eastward to Sconser, whence, in order 'to shun some very bad road', they took a boat over a dark and rainy sea with the boatmen singing very badly, like 'wild Indians'. Landing at Strol-lamus, they walked the two miles to Coirechatachan. There Donald Maclean of Coll ('young Coll'), who had offered his services as guide to the party at Talisker, and Lachlan Mackinnon of Coirechatachan and Boswell got very merry over three bowls of punch and Boswell had a hangover the next morning, when Johnson came into his room and said, 'What, drunk yet?' From Coirechatachan they went on the 28th to Ostaig and on 1 October they were back at Armadale. They left Armadale by boat for Mull, but a storm drove them off course and after a dangerous journey they landed on the island of Coll, where they stayed with young Coll in his comfortable but tradesman-like house on Breacacha Bay. There they were storm-bound until the 14th, when they sailed for Tobermory in Mull. On the 19th they landed on Iona ('Icolmkill') where they examined the ruins of the monastery and cathedral and Johnson was moved to historico-religious reflections. Next they went along the south shore of Mull to Lochbuie and from there on 22 October they took the primitive ferryboat to Oban. From there they rode south on small horses in tempestuous weather. At Inveraray they stayed at an inn, but were entertained to dinner by the Duke of Argyll, who ended what Johnson called their 'difficulties of peregrination' by providing excel-lent horses from his own stable. At Glasgow they were entertained by the professors of the University and then, with some trepidation, Boswell brought his substitute father (Tory and High Churchman) to his real father (Whig and staunch Presbyterian) at Auchinleck. On one occasion only did they clash, and Boswell 'was very much distressed by being present at an altercation between two men, both of whom I reverenced'. But, uncharacteristically, he refrained from writing down what they said, not wishing to exhibit his 'honoured father' and his 'respected friend as intellectual gladiators, for the entertainment of the public'. They were back in Edinburgh on 10 November. On 21 November Boswell accompanied Johnson to the inn at Blackshiels, fourteen miles south of Edinburgh, where they spent the night before Johnson boarded the London coach.

Even such a condensed catalogue of places as that just presented will give some idea of the strenuous nature of this Highland journey. For Boswell, it was the most memorable experience of his life. 'I was elated by the thought of having been enabled to entice such a man to this remote part of the world,' he wrote at Dunvegan. ' . . . I compared myself to a dog who had got hold of a large piece of meat, and runs

Dr Johnson in his 'travelling dress'. He was sixty-four at the time of this strenuous tour.

away with it to a corner, where he may devour it in peace, without any fear of others taking it from him.' It was at Dunvegan, too, that he noted down a defence of his propensity to accost any exalted person, whether he knew him or not. 'If I know myself, it is nothing more than an eagerness to share the society of men distinguished either by their rank or their talents, and a diligence to attain what I desire. If a man is praised for seeking knowledge, though mountains and seas are in his way, may he not be pardoned, whose ardour, in the pursuit of the same object, leads him to encounter difficulties as great, though of a different kind?' He had certainly gone through mountains and seas with Johnson, and both men acquired some notions of the traditions of Highland hospitality and the state of Highland culture of which both were previously ignorant. They found that culture much declined and decayed, but they could see for themselves that it still existed. They were sometimes elated, sometimes depressed. The

We have only Rowlandson's word for it that Johnson and Auchinleck, Tory and Whig, actually came to blows, but Boswell mentions 'an altercation between two men, both of whom I reverenced'.

weather was for the most part terrible. Boswell's own determined gaiety, his sociability, his readiness to sing or dance or drink with anybody, his continuous drawing out of Johnson and others in conversation, prevented any long lapses into depression or irritation, though there were such moments. Johnson himself revealed flashes of tenderness, generosity, light-heartedness, gratitude and high formal courtesy as well as impatience and irritation as he confronted different aspects of his new experience, and Boswell faithfully recorded them all. Mrs Boswell was glad to see the great man leave: his presence at James's Court, with the continuous entertaining and Johnson's own unpredictable habits, had been a great strain on her. Boswell returned from Blackshiels 'in a state of languor', worn out with having his mind 'kept on its utmost stretch' to keep Johnson entertained and to keep him performing properly.

Legal activity and correspondence with people he had met on the tour and with antiquaries and historians to get information for Johnson's account of the tour occupied much of his time the following winter. On 9 April he was deeply shocked to learn of Goldsmith's death. On 20 May his second daughter, Euphemia, was born, to whom he became scarcely less devoted than to Veronica. He had intended to spend the spring of 1774 in London, but he had no real reason to go, and Johnson discouraged his idea that he had an obligation to make an annual visit. He started his Journal again, after a gap, on 14 June 1774. On Saturday, 9 July he got riotously drunk with friends and awoke next morning 'half boiled with last night's debauch' and remorseful at having given his 'valuable spouse so much uneasiness'. On other days he recorded his 'complete sobriety and diligence'. He was engaged in a long quarrel with his father about inheritance; Boswell, believing in 'male dignity', did not believe in female succession to an estate and insisted that the Auchinleck estate should go, after him, to a male relative who was a dancing master rather than to a daughter of his own. But he felt unhappy at the injustice this might involve for his wife and daughters. He consoled himself with the thought that whatever happened his wife and daughters would be looked after.

On 1 August John Reid's second trial for sheep-stealing came on: this time he was accused of stealing nineteen sheep, driving them to his house and keeping them there and killing a certain number of them and selling the carcasses and skins. Reid's defence was that he received the sheep from one William Gardner and did not know them to be stolen. Gardner claimed, according to Reid, that he got the sheep from some horse-dealers. Gardner was now in prison at Stirling awaiting transportation for theft, and for various technical reasons his evidence could not be submitted, though a third party was brought forward to say that he knew there had been a bargain between Gardner and Reid. Boswell believed that there was a real possibility,

perhaps a probability, that Reid had received the sheep from Gardner in good faith, but also feared that Gardner's evidence might show Reid guilty of 'reset of theft' (receiving stolen goods); since this was punished by transportation rather than hanging, once Reid had been found guilty of the capital offence Boswell tried unavailingly to bring Gardner forward. But the trial really turned on the repeated affirmation by a number of witnesses and the agreement of the judges that Reid had a bad character and was 'by habit and repute' a thief. Boswell attributed this to the resentment of the judges at the jury's acquittal of Reid in 1766: they now persisted in regarding him as a man with a bad record although, as Boswell pointed out, 'the verdict of his country' had found him innocent on the only other occasion when he had been accused of a crime. But the allegation that Reid was a sheep-stealer 'by habit and repute' was freely bandied about in Court. True, Lord Auchinleck, one of the judges, admitted that habit and repute was not a crime, but 'when there is both habit and repute and a proof of the crime' then habit and repute was both an 'aggravation' and 'a

'Auchinleck does not signify *a stony field* as he [Dr Johnson] has said, but a *field of flagstones*; and this place has a number of rocks, which abound in strata of that kind.' Boswell took the Reverend Samuel Ogden's book, *Sermons on Prayer* (much admired by Johnson) with him on the Hebridean tour, and his mention of this fact in the *Journal* led to Rowlandson's several times showing it peeping from Boswell's pocket.

strong circumstance of guilt'. No modern court would have admitted any evidence of the implications of Reid's previous trial (and acquittal) and the reader today, on reading the proceedings, will probably believe that Reid would have been acquitted on the evidence if the case had come up in our own time. The jury, despite Boswell's eloquence, found Reid guilty at two o'clock the next day. The judges decided the offence was capital ('I'll own', said Lord Auchinleck, 'I think theft by our law a capital crime, more especially as here, where 'tis a *grex* [flock]') and Reid was sentenced to be hanged. Boswell tried every possible device first to delay the sentence and then, in an almost frenzied anxiety, to get some kind of pardon or reprieve, or a commutation of Reid's sentence to transportation. When all his attempts proved fruitless he even devised a hair-raising plan for a doctor to resuscitate Reid after he had been hanged and his body quickly removed to a secret place, but he gave that up before the execution. Reid was hanged on 21 September, Boswell pursuing him to the end with advice, religious consolation, and above all a consuming curiosity about his behaviour in the face of death and on the scaffold itself. Reid never confessed, and Boswell took this as final evidence of his innocence.

Boswell's Journal in the summer of 1774 projects his character with extraordinary vividness. Exerting himself for wretched clients in hopeless causes, engaging in periodic bouts of dissipation, reproaching himself for causing distress to his 'valuable friend', hugging to himself his moments of triumph or of happiness or of mere social calm, torturing himself with morbid imaginings or cheering himself with dreams of glory – it is a powerful and disturbing picture. 'I thought of lying in bed all forenoon and indulging in the humour in which I then was. I had a slight conflict between what I really thought would do me most good and the desire of being extremely decent and going to church.' 'There was very hard drinking. I however did not exceed a bottle and a half of old hock. But, with what I had at dinner, I was far gone.' 'I devoured moor-fowl, and poured more port down my throat. I was sadly intoxicated. *Perdidi diem.*' All this while he was frantically devising expedients to save John Reid. He came home after Reid's execution in a gloomy state. 'It was now about eight o'clock in the evening, and gloom came upon me. I went home and found my wife no comforter, as she thought I had carried my zeal for John too far, might hurt my own character and interest by it, and as she thought him guilty. I was so affrighted that I started every now and then and durst hardly rise from my chair at the fireside. I sent for Grange [John Johnston of Grange], but he was not at home. I however got Dr. Webster, who came and supped, and he and I drank a bottle of claret. But still I was quite dismal.'

As time went on, the contradictions in Boswell's life increased. He indulged in sporadic bouts of drinking, duly noted in his Journal. 'I

Boswell, his long-suffering wife and 'valuable friend', and his children.

was much intoxicated.' On 3 November, after drinking five bottles of claret with a friend, he 'raged through the streets' very drunk until he fell down a stone stair and bruised himself. Other social occasions were spirited without being drunken. 'Time passed very well. I lived fully and jolly.' His passion for gaming grew, and he lost considerable sums, in spite of promising his wife that he would 'never play at whist for more than a shilling the game and two shilling the rubber'. He worried intermittently about free-will and predestination. On 24 December he again roamed the streets very drunk and picked up two whores, only to feel ill and remorseful the next day. He continued to quarrel with his father on the matter of 'male succession' and maintaining his 'feudal resolution', until he agreed to a compromise in August 1776. He cherished his wife in spite of her 'being averse to hymeneal rites' and searched the Bible for evidence that concubinage was permitted. And yet he worked hard, indulged in religious meditations in church, and enjoyed serious and informed intellectual discussion with his friends.

General Paoli.

The Temple, seen from the Thames. Here, in 1775, Boswell started eating dinners with a view to being called to the English Bar.

In the spring of 1775 London called him again, and he left Edinburgh on 15 March, visiting his disturbed brother John at Newcastle on the way south. ('Poor man, my heart melted for him,' he wrote in his Journal. Boswell was never anything but tolerant and compassionate towards his deranged brother.) On arrival in London on the 21st he called on Johnson, who received him as kindly as ever. He also renewed his friendship with Dilly and, of course, with the great Paoli. He attended the Club and rejoiced in his association with the distinguished men there, though disgusted that a 'coarse and noisy' Scot called Fordyce had been elected a member. He reflected on his love of talking nonsense. ('To be perpetually talking sense runs out the mind, as perpetually ploughing and taking crops run out land. The mind must be manured, and nonsense is very good for the purpose.') He attended many a dinner- and supper-party, and occasionally got drunk. One day, looking for a 'Devonshire girl' for purposes of 'dalliance', he found instead 'the great lace-woman in Duke Street' and bought some lace for his wife, an unexpectedly virtuous act which gratified him immensely. On 23 April he left London for Mamhead, near Exeter, to stay with Temple, and while there he swore to Temple, under a venerable yew tree, that he would never drink more than six glasses at a time. He was back in London on 2 May, now staying with Paoli, as his landlord in the lodgings he had taken in Gerrard Street had let them to someone else in his absence. He renewed his friendship with Wilkes, now considered established

enough to consort with. And, in pursuance of his resolve to enter the English Bar, he started eating the prescribed dinners at the Inner Temple. He went with Johnson to the Thrales' villa at Streatham. By this time he had discovered, to his consternation, that Mrs Thrale was keeping a book of Johnsoniana, and he noted: 'I must try to get this *Thralian* Miscellany, to assist me in writing Mr. Johnson's Life, if Mrs. Thrale does not intend to do it herself.' But, though rivalry between Boswell and Mrs Thrale over Johnson was beginning to emerge, on the surface all was still amicability. On 22 May Boswell left London for Edinburgh.

Boswell reviewed his life 'during the summer session [12 June to 12 August] 1775' and pronounced it flat. 'My father's coldness to me, the unsettled state of our family affairs, and the poor opinion which I had of the profession of a lawyer in Scotland . . . sunk my spirits woefully; and for some of the last weeks of the session I was depressed with black melancholy.' He was having 'gloomy doubts' about a future state again. Yet he worked hard; 'wrote sixty papers', and earned a hundred and eighteen guineas and one pound. He became concerned about the war with America and (as he wrote to Temple) grew 'more and more an American' – in opposition to Johnson, who was firmly on the side of the British Government. On 9 October 1775 Boswell's son Alexander was born, and Boswell 'indulged some imaginations that he might be a great man'. A drunken evening on Saturday, 14 October was followed by attendance at church twice on the next day, 'so that I had a good counterbalance of decency' – a Boswell comment which is both illuminating and characteristic. Bouts of 'supine indolence' and compulsive gaming alternated with periods of hard work and moments (at least) of pious devotion. 'There are more pious minds than is believed to be. Many of my acquaintance would not think that I am devout.' Boswell was certainly devout at times, but in general he can better be described as someone who continually wanted to believe in religion and who hugged its comfort to him whenever he could work himself into a believing state of mind, than as a consistently devout person. He was continuously afraid of the victory of his own scepticism.

And so the Journal goes: drinking bouts, self-congratulation ('I am a man of old times'), bad temper ('in a sullen frame at supper with my wife'), near-delirium ('so furious that I took up the chairs in the dining-room and threw them about and broke some of them, and beat about my walking stick till I had it in pieces, and then put it into the fire and burnt it'), competent professional work ('I went on better with my business'), worry about his wife's health and consequent penitence and promise of reform (but 'my good practice is never of sufficiently long continuance to have a stable consistency. It is shaken loose by occasional repetitions of licentiousness'), more gaming, and all the time compulsive curiosity about himself ('But really I have a

Hester Thrale.

kind of strange feeling as if I wished nothing to be secret that concerns myself'). On 13 January 1776 he records that he has not tasted wine for a fortnight or dined or supped with anybody, but a few weeks later we find him both gaming and drinking again. On 10 February he was 'vexed' to think that he had not kept the vow he swore to Temple. 'My wife was so kind and engaging tonight, by exerting herself to relieve me from the foul fiend, that I was all love and gratitude', he recorded on 12 February. On 27 February, in a gloomy passion, he threw a guinea note into the fire because his wife had objected to his subscribing three shillings for a miscellany. (But he withdrew it before it was wholly burnt, and later 'got its value from the Royal Bank'.) On 7 March he traced in detail 'the original and progress of a debauch of which I am ashamed'. By March his thoughts were turning once again to a spring trip to London, and he actually managed to enlist his stepmother's support in trying to persuade his father that these trips were proper and necessary. At the same time he was working himself up into a terrible state because, believing that something the Lord Advocate (Henry Dundas) had said was an insult to his father, he had written him a letter which might be construed as a challenge, and he worried himself sick about fighting a duel. Eventually the matter was cleared up to the satisfaction of all parties, but this was not the first, nor was it to be the last, time that Boswell got himself involved almost to the point of fighting a duel. (By a strange coincidence, Boswell's son Alexander was to be killed

'A Scene in Islington Fields.' With Boswell, affairs never quite reached this pitch, but more than once he came to the brink.

in a duel.) But when he left for London on 11 March he was still deeply worried about the prospect of a duel and took leave of his 'valuable spouse' with an earnest embrace and the words, 'God grant we may meet in a better world!'

In London he promptly went to see Johnson, whom he found now removed from Johnson's Court to Bolt Court. He called on Paoli, who received him 'with the most benignant complacency and kindness'. He met Charles Fox, 'who was indifferently civil'. At first he drank wine only moderately and 'felt a calm and gay felicity'. He went to Oxford with Johnson and shared a room with him at the Angel Inn, which reminded Boswell of their Hebridean journey. In Oxford he 'felt that kind of consolatory respectful frame' which that university city always produced in him. They met and talked with a variety of scholars, including Thomas Warton where the conversation (the high spots of which were as usual recorded by Boswell) turned to Sir Richard Steele's morals and this turned Boswell's mind to his favourite subject of 'patriarchal extensiveness'. He noted that he had had 'two late visits to an amorous lady in London' and wanted desperately to believe that such behaviour was justifiable. The next day, when Johnson advised various recreations and 'retreats for [his] mind as a cure for melancholy', Boswell '*thought* of concubinage, but was afraid to mention it'.

By this time Johnson and Boswell were on their way to Birmingham, where Johnson visited an old schoolfellow. They went on to Lichfield, Johnson's birthplace, where Boswell met Johnson's stepdaughter, Lucy Porter, and Garrick's elder brother. At Lichfield Cathedral on Sunday, 24 March Boswell enjoyed the solemn music, but 'sensual connexions with women' (especially the amorous lady in London) moved his thoughts to sex, and he thought of 'Asiatic satisfactions, quite consistent with devotion and with a fervent attachment to my valuable spouse'. The next day Johnson rebuked him smartly for his persistent questioning and for trying to draw him out about details of his earlier life. From Lichfield they went to visit Dr John Taylor in Ashbourne, Derbyshire, and they were back in London on 29 March, where he at once got drunk and, not finding his amorous lady at home, 'in a kind of brutal fever, went to the Park, and was relieved by dalliance'. A further bottle of claret after that was followed by further 'dalliance', and finally, when he was returning late to Paoli's, where he was staying, he was 'picked up by a strumpet at the head of St. James's Street' and in his 'drunken venturousness' had intercourse with her too. He got back to Paoli's between three and four in the morning. The next morning he was attacked by hangover and remorse. But this did not prevent him from picking up another girl in the Park that afternoon, after which he 'dined at General Paoli's and drank coffee comfortably'. More fierce drinking and wenching followed on subsequent days.

Dr Johnson's house in Bolt Court, off Fleet Street.

Again and again during his frequent meetings with Johnson during this period in London Boswell tried to get the great man to give a favourable opinion about concubinage and extra-marital sexual satisfactions, but Johnson would not be drawn and in the end Johnson seems to have shut him up on the subject. By mid-April Boswell's behaviour had settled into a less violent routine. 'I supped at Lord Mountstuart's. My mind for these several days was placid and gay.' Boswell's greatest triumph as an observer and, one might almost say, manipulator of Johnson was his managing to arrange that Johnson should accept on 15 May an invitation to dinner where John Wilkes (whom Johnson detested on principle and had never met) was also a guest. The device was a brilliant success: Johnson and Wilkes, in spite of their vast differences in principle and temperament, took to each other, and Boswell later recorded their amiable conversation with supreme satisfaction. As remarkable in its way was Boswell's success in achieving and recording an interview with the criminal adventuress and courtesan Margaret Caroline Rudd, now living alone in Queen Street. He wrote, but did not send, a long letter to his wife describing in minute detail his long interview with this extraordinary woman. Boswell left London for Edinburgh on 16 May 1776. On that day Johnson wrote to Mrs Boswell: 'You will now have Mr. Boswell home; it is well that you have him; he has led a wild life.'

The return to the Edinburgh routine, as so often, depressed Boswell. In his Journal in the summer of 1776 we find recurring phrases such as 'averse to labour', 'ill', 'averse to business', 'sadly low spirited', 'indolent, listless, and gloomy'. His famous visit to the dying Hume in July stirred his lurking religious scepticism, and it must always be remembered that scepticism was something Boswell dreaded and fought against in great distress of mind. The day before Hume's funeral he got very drunk and picked up a whore on the streets, telling his wife as soon as he got home. Yet interspersed with these records of depression and abandon we find quieter moments of family affection, professional activity, and normal social life. On 3 October he noted his contented state of mind, congratulated himself on some skilful legal work, and wondered how he had been so 'gloomy, listless, and desponding' in the summer, and on the 17th he noted his 'good, steady, and cheerful spirits'. He saw his father frequently, at Edinburgh or at Auchinleck, and had his moments of concern and affection as well as of irritation.

On 15 November his son David was born: he was a sickly infant from the start and survived only until 29 March 1777. The day after the birth he 'snatched a little romping pleasure' from Annie Cunninghame, a teenage orphaned niece of his wife's who was spending some time with the Boswells and to whom Boswell, much to his wife's uneasiness, was physically attracted. On 27 November, a bitterly

This portrait of Boswell was painted by Sir Joshua Reynolds, a fellow member of The Club, in 1785.

cold night, after much drink he picked up 'a plump hussy who called herself Peggy Grant' and 'boldly lay with her' in a field behind the Register Office. (Most of his Edinburgh whorings were done in the open air, sometimes in the oddest places.) The next day he spoke in court 'with much gravity and dull attention' for nearly two hours. His head filled with thoughts of Peggy Grant in the midst of his legal business, he 'was shocked that the father of a family should go among strumpets', but comforted himself with thoughts of the Patriarchs. He found Peggy Grant again on 1 December, 'lay with her twice' in a shed in St Andrew's Square, came home and confessed to his wife, who was 'very uneasy' while he was 'ashamed and vexed'. But, he adds, his conscience was not troubled, since he had persuaded himself that such indulgence was permitted.

And so the record goes, up and down, sober and drunk, busy and idle, satisfied and deeply gloomy, a loving husband and devoted father and a chaser of whores. In January he recorded 'a kind of *faintness of mind*, a total indifference as to all objects of whatever kind, united with a melancholy dejection' and he brooded over death. He had been attending rather a lot of funerals and hearing of a lot of deaths. On 16 March he records that he had achieved philosophical calm and was happy, and this seems to have marked the beginning of a better period. At Auchinleck on the 22nd he got on well with his father. Even the death of little David made him tender and sentimental rather than melancholy, and a few days later he was in the highest spirits, reporting 'a delightful day' with his work going well and the sun shining brightly. On 14 April he congratulated himself on his sound and vigorous state and his confidence in life after death. At Auchinleck a fortnight later he found his father 'more failed' than when he had last seen him and was struck 'with affectionate concern and with a depression of mind', but the mood did not last. In the circuit court at Jedburgh in May he conducted a complicated legal case 'to full satisfaction'. Bouts of intoxication and whoring are recorded in his notes in the summer (when he kept no journal), and these were not notably diminished by his anxiety about the health of his wife, who was showing the first symptoms of what proved to be tuberculosis. The Boswells had by now moved from James's Court to a house with a garden on the south side of The Meadows, the park well to the south of the Old Town of Edinburgh (not to the north,

The Meadows, with the Castle in the background looking deceptively near.

Ashbourne church – 'one of the largest and most luminous that I have seen', Boswell wrote in his Journal.

where the New Town was being developed) which had been laid out on the site of the drained Burgh Loch.

On 10 September Boswell set out for Ashbourne, to see Johnson who was then there. He was now keeping his Journal again, and he noted that his wife did not think he had sufficient reason for leaving her and the children and did not realize that his visit 'to meet an exalted instructor' could be compared to a pilgrimage to a sacred place. He had moments of sadness and remorse (as well as of lasciviousness) on the way, but, once with Johnson, he became more and more involved in drawing out and listening to his hero, though his 'dilatory notation' prevented his recording much of Johnson's conversation in his Journal. But he did record a fair amount, including an incident on 22 September when Boswell revealed his hand too unguardedly in saying he would like to see Johnson and Mrs Catharine Macaulay, the Whig historian whose republican views Johnson scorned, together. 'No, Sir. You would not see us quarrel to make you sport. Don't you see that it is very uncivil to pit two people against one another?' Johnson did not realize that Boswell had already done that with him and Wilkes, although the consequence was not in fact a quarrel. On 27 September Boswell was back in his Edinburgh house in Meadow Lane.

It was in October 1777, after his return from Ashbourne, that Boswell started writing essays for *The London Magazine* under the revealing pseudonym of 'The Hypochondriack'. The first of these

THE LONDON MAGAZINE:

Or, GENTLEMAN's Monthly Intelligencer.

For NOVEMBER, 1782.

With the following Embellishments, viz.

An elegant Engraving of the Right Honourable HENRY DUNDAS,

AND

A curious Plate of new-invented WATER-ENGINES.

LONDON, printed for R. BALDWIN, at No. 47, in Pater-noster-Row.
Of whom may be had complete Sets, from the Year 1732 to the present Time, ready bound
and stitched, or any single Volume to complete Sets.

forty contributions appeared in the October 1777 issue of the magazine, and the last in August 1783. These essays, though highly personal in tone, have not the compulsive autobiographical note of his Journal; they are ordered reflections, with many illustrations from his own experience and observation, about human moods, hopes and fears, habits and institutions, in tone, one might say, midway between Montaigne and Charles Lamb. The titles themselves are revealing: they include 'On Fear', 'On Hypochondria' (two), 'On Conscience', 'On Reserve', 'On Drinking' (three), 'On Marriage', 'On Ridicule', 'On Diaries', 'On Memory'. The writing of the essays was in a sense therapeutic for Boswell, driving away melancholy by writing about it or about some other cause of human anxiety or concern. In his concluding essay Boswell wrote that he knew that in future he would 'view these papers with relish or dissatisfaction, in different states of his mind'. He had long known himself well enough to be aware of the drastic ups and downs of his own moods. To share these and discussions of the problems which bore on them with other people was one part of his purpose in writing the essays; another part was to control and discipline them by finding an 'objective correlative' of them as a subject to write about. And of course there were also his love of writing and of being published and his desire to make money by writing, which had been with him since he was a very young man.

In January 1778 Boswell was frightened by his wife's spitting blood and described himself as being also 'very ill'. She improved in a few weeks and Boswell celebrated her recovery by getting drunk and picking up prostitutes in the street. Then she had a relapse, and this, combined with the news of Lady Eglinton's death in her early twenties, changed his mood again: he 'felt universal indifference' and considered his wife's death, his own, or anybody else's, of no significance. Better moods prevailed in the spring and, his wife's condition no longer giving cause for anxiety (though his earlier behaviour had led to a 'state of coolness' between them), he decided to make another of his regular jaunts to London. Characteristically, he determined to break down his wife's coolness by more prudent behaviour while for the time being reflecting that it made parting from her less painful. But at the actual parting on 13 March Mrs Boswell was 'very tender', while 'Veronica cried much and clasped her little arms round my neck, calling out "O Papá!"' Boswell was in London from 17 March to 28 May. He stayed with Paoli.

On arrival in London Boswell found to his disappointment that Johnson was in Streatham with the Thrales, but he was back on 20 March and Boswell called on him to resume their old relationship. He was now 'drinking only water' and was 'quiet and happy'. His feeling for Johnson was stronger than ever. 'I really *worshipped* him, not idolatrously, but with profound reverence.' He called on Lord Mountstuart, Lord Eglinton, his father's old friend and his own

(*Opposite*) Contents page of *The London Magazine*, for which Boswell, disguised as 'The Hypochondriack', wrote essays.

valued counsellor Sir John Pringle, and many other old friends and acquaintances. He met Wilkes again, and found him 'the same cheerful, gay, polite, classical man as when he and I were happy together at Naples in 1765'. He was enormously proud of himself for sticking to water, and made a point of raising the subject often with Johnson (who had himself been a water-drinker for quite some time). He recorded at length a memorable evening at the Club on 3 April, when Johnson, Burke, the young R.B. Sheridan, Sir Joshua Reynolds, Gibbon and Boswell himself indulged in wide-ranging conversation with the topics including the sculpting of animals, emigration, the House of Commons, the Irish language, taxes, travel literature, happiness, and wine. Boswell was 'very happy', and was more and more determined to settle in London. At the same time, as he told Garrick, he was 'an old Scot, proud of being descended of ancestors who have had an estate for some hundreds of years'. He had a few adventures with a woman he calls in his Journal '36' and who may have been Mrs Love, but on the whole this period in London was in sharp contrast with his visit of 1776: this time Boswell was sober, agreeably sociable, and on the whole happy.

Mrs Boswell was now pregnant again, and (as is quite common in cases of tuberculosis) the symptoms of her illness disappeared during

A meeting of the Literary Club at Sir Joshua Reynolds's house shows (left to right) Boswell, Johnson, Reynolds, David Garrick, Edmund Burke, Paoli, Dr Burney, Tom Warton and Goldsmith.

her pregnancy. The baby, a boy whom they called James, was born on 15 September 1778. The following January Boswell wrote to Johnson that he was 'exceedingly well, and the better of drinking wine sometimes'. He was saddened by Garrick's death during the same month, but does not seem to have given way to one of his moods of real melancholia, though he continued to be subject to such moods intermittently. Johnson was continually exhorting him to drive away fits of 'anxiety, or gloominess, or perversion of mind' by not talking of them openly and keeping himself busy. His most effective way of banishing these moods was, however, a visit to London, and he went again in the spring of 1779, arriving on 15 March and finding lodgings in South Audley Street. For reasons which he does not explain, Boswell was 'unaccountably negligent in preserving Johnson's sayings, more so than at any time' when he was regularly in his company, but his negligence was relative and he preserved a fair number of significant fragments. On 19 March he was with Johnson and the Thrales at Streatham. On 31 March he confessed to Johnson that he had succumbed to a rage for gambling and sat up a whole night playing cards. He of course saw Paoli and Reynolds and other of his friends in London. On 16 April he attended the trial of one Hackman, who 'in a fit of frantick jealous love' had shot his sweetheart after she

(*Left*) Sir Joshua Reynolds, a self-portrait.

(*Right*) Samuel Johnson, a portrait by John Opie painted in 1783. The day after this portrait was painted, Johnson had a stroke; he died in December of the following year.

had been taken up by a nobleman. On 26 April, laid up with an inflamed foot, he sent a note to Johnson who, to his immense gratification, came with Sir Joshua Reynolds and talked at his bedside. On 1 May Boswell was finally able to bring Johnson to visit the seventy-one-year-old Earl of Marchmont, who had been a close friend of Pope and who could therefore tell Johnson much that would be of interest to him for his account of Pope in his *Lives of the Poets*. He had tried in vain to bring the two together on a previous visit, when Johnson had expressed no interest at all. Now Johnson was delighted with his two-hour interview, saying that he 'would rather have given twenty pounds than not have come'. On 3 May Boswell set out on his return journey to Scotland after dining with Johnson at Dilly's.

As so often on his return to Edinburgh from London, Boswell was depressed by the contrast between life in London and life in the Scottish capital. He felt 'a supine indolence of mind' which lasted through much of the summer and was only dissipated when he got an opportunity to visit London again at the end of September. His friend Colonel James Stuart asked Boswell to accompany him to Leeds and then to London on a military mission. He arrived in London at the beginning of October and left on the 18th, seeing much of Johnson. He visited Lichfield on his way home to Scotland and, anxious as always to increase his knowledge of Johnson's background, talked of Johnson to his friends there as he had done on his earlier visit with the great man himself. He was now pretty determined to write Johnson's biography, a project which he had first definitely referred to as early as November 1775 in a letter to Temple. From Lichfield he went on to Chester (still with Colonel Stuart), where, as he wrote to Johnson, he felt unusually happy, and then went on to Carlisle where he reported to his mentor that '*the black dog* that worries me at home I cannot but dread'. In reply, Johnson urged him to 'get rid of all intellectual excesses' and exaggerate neither his pleasures nor his vexations. 'Why should you not be as happy at Edinburgh as at Chester?' It was a crucial question, and Boswell himself was uncertain of the answer.

A partial explanation of Boswell's moods of depression at this time was his increasing frustration in his political ambitions which, far from having given up, he nursed ever more eagerly. Every time an office to which he thought he could aspire fell vacant, he wrote to somebody of real or supposed influence to try and get it. Lord Mountstuart (with whom he had long ago made up the quarrel they had in Italy) was someone he frequently turned to. In November 1775 he had written to Mountstuart asking him for his help in securing the 'office of one of the Commissaries of Edinburgh' made vacant by the death of James Smollet, and reminding him that they had talked of 'a much better thing – Baron Maule's office of Clerk to the Register of Sasines' and Mountstuart had promised to get help

A view of Edinburgh, 1790. The New Town is at top right.

from the Duke of Queensberry in this project. But someone else was appointed Commissary, and John Maule, a Baron of the Court of Exchequer in Scotland, lived on in that office until 1781. Mountstuart said that he and Queensberry would get something else for Boswell, but nothing happened. Boswell kept on at Mountstuart, but got nothing but vague promises and a loan of £100. (Boswell was not now doing especially well at the Bar in Edinburgh, and felt the need of a salaried office strongly.)

Disappointed in Mountstuart, he tried to heal his breach with Henry Dundas and his elder brother Robert, the Lord President. When Boswell was at Auchinleck early in 1780 visiting his father, who was ill, he took the opportunity to call on Henry Dundas at his estate at Melville. In the spring he dined at Arniston with Robert Dundas, who shook hands with him as he left and said, 'My dear James, nobody wishes you better than I do.' Lord Auchinleck was pleased at the reconciliation, and for the moment Boswell was happy. But the reconciliation was uncertain and in any case it had no concrete results, and Boswell became gloomy again. He threw himself into the Ayrshire parliamentary election of October 1780: though his aim was to secure the seat one day for himself, his strategy at this time led him to support Major Hugh Montgomerie while Dundas and Lord Auchinleck supported Sir Adam Fergusson. Montgomerie won, to

Robert Dundas, Lord President of the Court of Session and (*below*) his younger brother Henry, Viscount Melville. Boswell's reconciliation with them led to none of the hoped-for advantage.

Boswell's joy, but on appeal to the Court of Session for a review of the freeholders' votes (the voting system in rural Scotland at that time being based on a definition of a county freeholder that lent itself to manipulation) Fergusson was declared the winner.

Boswell tried to find new sources of influence. He tried to get Paoli to suggest to the King that Boswell wished to serve near him; he wrote to Burke saying how pleasant it would be if the King decided to 'transplant' him to London (but he agreed that this was probably a 'romantick vision'); he sought an interview with the old and retired Lord Bute, not, he insisted (somewhat disingenuously) for help in his political career but simply for the privilege of talking with a great man: he obtained the interview in May 1781, but it did him no good. The following year, to quote from an anonymous memoir of himself that Boswell wrote for the *European Magazine and London Review* in 1791, 'when Mr Burke was in power [having become Paymaster of the Forces when Lord Rockingham became Prime Minister on the resignation of Lord North] that celebrated Gentleman shewed his sense of Mr Boswell's merit in the warmest manner, observing "We must do something for you for our own sakes", and recommended him to General Conway for a vacant place, by a letter in which his character was drawn in glowing colours. The place was not obtained; but Mr. Boswell declared, that he valued the letter more.' Boswell had mixed feelings about the Rockingham administration, feeling that his 'Tory or monarchical enthusiasm' did not 'perfectly accord' with its principles, but he was desperate for influence and was willing to try anybody. Burke advised Boswell to stick to Henry Dundas, and Boswell once again sought him out and achieved a new reconciliation of sorts, but the only consequence was that Dundas professed friendship in non-committal terms. Dundas pointed out that it would cost Boswell about £3,000 to buy a seat in Parliament and advised that he cultivate his law practice with a view to establishing a claim to a judgeship which Dundas could support. Boswell could not accept what he considered this limited horizon.

Boswell was unable to see Johnson in 1780. He urged that they should meet in the north of England so that the year would not go by without a meeting, but Johnson was too much involved with the Thrales, who were going through an anxious time because of Mr Thrale's parliamentary activities when he was in fact a dying man. 'This year must pass without an interview,' Johnson wrote firmly to Boswell on 17 October 1780. The best Johnson could do was try to help Boswell out of his fits of gloom. 'I hoped you had got rid of all this hypocrisy of misery,' he wrote to him on 14 March 1781. 'What have you to do with Liberty and Necessity? Or what more than to hold your tongue about it? Do not doubt but I shall be most heartily glad to see you here again, for I love every part about you but your affectation of distress.' This was just before Boswell left for London,

'A London Chop House': the two diners caricatured in the foreground are Boswell and Johnson.

for he did manage a visit in spring 1781, arriving in London on 19 March and seeing Johnson the next day. In London Boswell's spirits soared. On 20 April he spent with Johnson what he described as 'one of the happiest days that I remember to have enjoyed in the whole course of my life'. On 8 May he dined once again with Johnson and Wilkes at Mr Dilly's. 'No *negociation* was now required to bring them together; for Johnson was so well satisfied with his former interview, that he was very glad to meet Wilkes again.' Boswell dined many times with Johnson before leaving London on 2 June. Johnson came with him as far as Southill, Bedfordshire, where they visited a brother of Mr Dilly. It was at Southill that, 'being in a frame of mind which, I hope for the felicity of human nature, many experience, – in fine weather, – at the country-house of a friend, – consoled and elevated by pious exercises', he made a supreme effort to get Johnson to make a comprehensive statement about religion that would set his mind at rest once and for all. Johnson did make a remarkable statement (which did not, of course, permanently soothe Boswell), but prefaced it by warning Boswell against trusting to *impressions*. 'There is a middle state of mind between conviction and hypocrisy, of which many are unconscious. By trusting to impressions, a man may gradually come to yield to them, and at length be subject to them, so as not to be a free agent, or what is the same thing in effect, to *suppose* that he is not a free agent.' On 5 June they parted, Boswell resuming his journey north to Edinburgh.

As 1781 moved into 1782 Boswell found much to be gloomy about. His wife was now clearly consumptive and both she and Boswell

months been afflicted with a hoarse[ness] and pain in her breast at times, and has upon three different occasions spit some blood. These are symptoms very alarming to her, because that dismal disease a Consumption has been fatal in her family her brother and all her sisters having died of it. I flatter myself that her complaints are occasioned by a severe cold joined with nervous illness, and that when the weather grows mild, she will recover her health. You may figure, My Dear Sir, how dreary a State I should be in were she to die & leave me with three young children. I beg to have your

worried about what he would do if left alone with five children (the youngest, Elizabeth, known as 'Betsy', had been born in 1780). On 5 January 1782 Johnson wrote to report that his own health had been 'tottering' and to express the hope that Mrs Boswell would 'surmount her complaints'. Lord Auchinleck was also ill, and clearly failing. Boswell hoped to cheer himself by visiting London in the spring, but Johnson wrote firmly saying they must be content to miss each other's company that spring. 'You have not lost much by missing my company,' Johnson wrote him on 3 June; 'I have scarcely been well for a single week.' Boswell himself was ill with influenza in the latter part of June and early July, while his wife was spitting blood as well as suffering from swelling, sweats and shooting pains. By early July

our prayers for her preservation.

I have occasion to be in London about the 24th of next month. I wish [to] prevail with her to accompany me, but she dislikes travelling; and prefers going to some country place in Scotland where she can have her children along with her. Perhaps however, she may yield to intreaty.

I hope Lady Rothes & your young ones are well. I had the pleasure of seeing your mother & sister for a few minutes last autumn at Ashbourne where I had a cordial meeting with Dr Johnson. How does the Club go on? and how is Mr Beauclerc? My Wife joins me in best compliments to you & Lady Rothes and I ever am Dear Sir, your most obedt humble servant
James Boswell

A letter from Boswell to Bennet Langton shows his anxiety about his wife's health, and about 'how dreary a state I should be in were she to die & leave me with three young children'. The letter was written in February 1778; Mrs Boswell was subsequently able to increase his anxieties by two.

Mrs Boswell was somewhat better, and Boswell himself felt completely recovered on 8 July. He was cheered by a letter from Mrs Thrale reporting that Johnson, too, had improved. Nevertheless, this was an unhappy time for him. The hope of making up for his lost spring visit to London by a journey in August was dashed by his father's worsening condition: Lord Auchinleck died on 30 August. Boswell, at forty-two, was now Laird of Auchinleck and freed at last from that constant sense of inferiority and dependence that he always felt with respect to his father.

'You, dear Sir, have now a new station, and have therefore new cares, and new employments,' wrote Johnson to Boswell on hearing of Auchinleck's death. He dissuaded Boswell from hastening to see him in London. Boswell, however, was determined to get his mentor's advice in person on his future course of action. He set out for London on 24 September, but returned the next day on being brought news that his wife 'had a violent fit of spitting blood'. By December Mrs Boswell was sufficiently improved to be able to write to Johnson herself telling him that she was better and expressing the hope that she would see him again in Scotland. Boswell, meanwhile, was redoubling his efforts to achieve a political appointment. He delivered a speech at Ayr Quarter Sessions attacking Scottish political abuses and made himself active in the movement for reform of the voting system in Scotland. In London the political situation was now extremely fluid. The formation of the Fox–North coalition in 1783, though it brought into power a ministry with whose principles and personalities Boswell had no sympathy, excited him with its prospect of new sources of influence. And Lord Mountstuart had returned to London after a period as Envoy in Turin, and so, Boswell hoped, was again available to use his influence on his behalf. With optimistic visions of a seat in Parliament ahead of him, or at the very least a Scottish judgeship (he now accepted this as a possible if minimal objective), he set off for London and arrived on 20 March 1783.

Mountstuart gave Boswell advice, but no practical help, and this spring visit to London proved as politically fruitless as so many others had been. He cheered himself with a consciousness of his new dignity as Laird of Auchinleck and fancied that both Johnson and Mrs Thrale (at whose house in Argyll Street Johnson was staying when Boswell arrived) appreciated him more for this reason. Johnson himself 'looked pale, and was distressed with a difficulty of breathing'. When he met Johnson at Mrs Thrale's house, Johnson said, 'I am glad you are come: I am very ill.' Shortly afterwards Mrs Thrale left for Bath, and she and Boswell never met again. They were henceforth to be increasingly enemies, though at a distance. With Johnson his relationship was as cordial as ever and in spite of his poor health the seventy-four-year-old sage spoke with his characteristic lively didacticism on the many occasions when Boswell was with him. 'You must be as much with me as you can. You have done me good,' he told him. Boswell confided his parliamentary ambitions to Johnson, who replied that unless he entered Parliament resolved to support any administration he would be the worse off, for he would have to live more expensively. Boswell left London for Scotland on 30 May, spending part of the 29th with Johnson and parting from him 'in more than usual earnestness; as his health was in a more precarious state than at any time when I had parted from him'.

Back in Scotland, Boswell continued his campaign to obtain political office. When in August 1783 Fox dismissed Henry Dundas as Lord Advocate, Boswell wrote to Burke asking his help in obtaining the post of Lord Advocate or of Solicitor-General; Burke

replied that he would do what he could but he had lost all influence with the important people in government and had little hope of being able to achieve anything. The position of Lord Advocate in fact went to Henry Erskine, a leader of the anti-Dundas group in Scotland and brother of the Earl of Buchan, while Alexander Wight was appointed Solicitor-General. Boswell wrote angrily to Burke of the 'total neglect which I have had the mortification to experience, at a time when I had reason to think and when it was generally thought that I could not fail to receive some mark of attention from the administration'. The defeat of Fox's East India Bill in December led to the collapse of the Fox–North coalition and the coming to power of William Pitt the Younger. Boswell, who had always had reservations about Fox, turned to the new Pitt ministry for support in his ambitions. He wrote to the Earl of Pembroke and to Lord Mountstuart for help in obtaining the position of Solicitor-General in the new administration and he entered politics as a pamphleteer.

The pamphlet he produced was entitled *A Letter to the People of Scotland on the Present State of the Nation*; in it Boswell urged the

Boswell and the widowed Mrs Thrale, both jealous Johnsonians, became increasingly enemies. Here their enmity is unkindly caricatured; Gabriele Piozzi, soon to marry the wealthy and attractive widow, watches nervously.

The powerful brothers Henry and Robert Dundas.

Scottish people to address the King and express their pleasure at the defeat of Fox's East India Bill. The pamphlet succeeded in obtaining addresses to the King which, according to Boswell, 'had much effect', and Pitt himself congratulated Boswell on his 'zealous and able exertions in the cause of the public'. The pamphlet was certainly well received, and its main arguments – that Fox's Bill would have violated both the property rights of the East India Company and the Constitution – were widely repeated. Boswell continued his activities in promoting addresses to the King, including a powerful one from Ayrshire in March 1784. Then he set out for London confident of obtaining there his political reward. He got as far as York, where he organized another address, but hearing there that Parliament had been dissolved he returned to Edinburgh to prepare for active participation in the Ayrshire election. The electoral situation in Ayrshire was confused; after believing that he himself would be able to stand as a candidate Boswell learned that Hugh Montgomerie, who had a prior claim and to whom he was committed, was standing again after all, so Boswell had to direct his energies towards canvassing for Montgomerie. In his address 'To the real freeholders of the County of Ayr' he described himself as 'a steady Royalist, who reveres monarchy, but is at the same time animated with genuine feelings of liberty'. He renewed contact with Dundas (now, under Pitt, more powerful than ever) and wrote a poem in honour of both Dundas and the candidate for the city of Edinburgh, James Hunter-Blair, stanzas from which were printed in the newspapers. All this, however, brought Boswell's political ambitions no nearer realization.

Boswell was in London again after the election, arriving on 5 May 1784, and he found Johnson 'greatly recovered'. He went with Johnson to Oxford on 3 June and returned to London on the 19th. On 22 June he dined with Johnson at the Club, 'the last time of his being in that respectable society'. That same day Boswell 'was present at the shocking sight of fifteen men executed before Newgate'. On 30 June, dining with Johnson at Sir Joshua Reynolds's house, Boswell had his last conversation with Johnson. He accompanied him back to Bolt Court. 'We bade adieu to each other affectionately in the carriage. When he had got down upon the foot-pavement, he called out, "Fare you well;" and without looking back, sprung away with a kind of pathetick briskness, if I may use that expression, which seemed to indicate a struggle to conceal uneasiness, and impressed me with a foreboding of our long, long separation.' Johnson died the following December.

With Johnson's death Boswell lost not only the man he most admired in the world and the man whose advice, support and friendship (even when he did not follow the advice) nourished his self-respect, but also the man with reference to whom his talents for productive and stimulating companionship could be most fully

employed. In drawing out Johnson, in enjoying and, in an innocent way, exploiting Johnson's genuine affection for him, Boswell found rich use for aspects of his own character which henceforth found no adequate employment. The writing of Johnson's biography was to prove a long and difficult process, in spite of the abundant materials he had already gathered. Immediately after Johnson's death Charles Dilly wrote to Boswell asking if he could have a four-hundred-page octavo volume of Johnson's sayings ready by February (i.e. in less than two months), but Boswell made it clear that he had much material and would write Johnson's biography with deliberation. 'I was now uneasy', he noted, 'to think that there would be considerable expectations from me of Memoirs of my illustrious Friend; but that habits of indolence and dejection of spirit would probably hinder me from laudable exertion. I wish I could write now, as when I wrote my *Account of Corsica*.'

His Journal from now on records his laborious sorting and collecting of Johnsonian material and then his writing of it (in London), with intervals of incapacity or indolence or dissipation for which he reproached himself. His correspondence shows how indefatigably he pursued anyone who could possibly provide some authentic

An execution before Newgate – 'a shocking sight' according to Boswell – was always a well-attended spectacle.

information about Johnson. Lucy Porter, Johnson's stepdaughter; Dr John Taylor of Ashbourne; William Gerard Hamilton, an important parliamentary figure whose conversational powers had been highly praised by Johnson; Thomas Warton, the poet and historian of English poetry; Bishop Percy, the editor and antiquary; and Johnson's friend and fellow member of the Literary Club Bennet Langton, all contributed useful material. The critic and scholar Edmund Malone gave valuable advice on organization, method and style as well as practical help in revising the manuscript and correcting proofs. He was also much helped by the essayist and politician (and member of the Club) John Courtenay. In May 1787 Boswell announced in the newspapers that the reason for the delay in publication of his *Life of Johnson* was that he had been awaiting the appearance of other publications from which he expected to derive information. The book was finally published on 16 May 1791.

Dedicated though he was to writing the life of his 'illustrious friend', this was very far from Boswell's sole interest in the years after Johnson's death. His father's death had liberated him to pursue a political career more fiercely than ever, and the story of the last twelve years of his life is in part the story of his increasingly desperate attempts in this direction. His wife's health gave him continual worry, until her death in June 1789. He had his usual recurring bouts of deep depression. And the familiar story of periodic outbursts of drunkenness and picking up prostitutes went on. He would seek to relieve his moods of depression by a variety of social activities, and time and again we find him at some dinner-party drinking too much and talking too excitedly, wondering the next morning what he had said the night before, reproaching himself for having been 'wretchedly dissipated', promising himself amendment. Gradually, in spite of his feverish pursuit of a political career, he came to realize, largely under Malone's influence, that the *Life of Johnson* would be his real claim to fame. Malone, he recorded on 1 May 1788, 'lectured me upon my intemperance, and on my delaying Johnson's *Life*, on which I was to rest my fame'. In June 1790 he wrote to Malone that it was shocking that he had been forced to interrupt work on the *Life*, which he described as 'the most important, perhaps *now* the only concern of any consequence that I ever shall have in this world'.

At the time of Johnson's death Boswell was again in touch with Dundas about his political future. Dundas, finding that Boswell had only £500 a year free, instead of £1,000 or more that he had believed, expressed doubt about the advisability of his going to the English Bar, and promised to use his influence with Pitt and others to get him a place of some hundreds a year. Boswell should not, he advised, try for a judgeship at once, for once a judge he could obtain no further office; he would be better off if he could obtain a sinecure before going to the Bench. Boswell believed Dundas 'sincere', though his wife

~~Samuel Johnson~~ was born at Lichfield × on the 18th of Septem:ber N.S. 1709 × His Father was Michael Johnson ~~a~~ ‡ who settled in Lichfield as a Book:seller ~~and Stationer~~. His Mother was Sarah Ford, descended of an ancient race of substantial yeomanry in Warwickshire. They were well advanced in years when they married, and never had more than ~~only~~ two children both sons; Samuel ~~and~~ their first born, who ~~[illegible]~~ lived to be the ~~great man whom~~ illustrious character ~~in his own age~~ ~~that I am humbly~~ whose various excellence I am to endeavour to record, and Nathanael, who died in his twenty fifth year.

Mr. Michael Johnson was a man of a large and robust body and of a strong and active mind; yet

‡ native of Derbyshire, of obscure extraction

× May I not say 18th and put a note mentioning that according to the computation of time which then obtained his birth day was supposed to be the 7th. But as the computation was eleven days short of the truth, and has been corrected by general authority I think it best to put it right.

‡ Where shall the epitaphs on his Father mother and brother be inserted? I suppose in notes.

remained sceptical: in the event, nothing happened. Boswell was sanguine enough to believe that Montgomerie, whom he had helped in the Ayrshire election, would be given a political appointment and would then resign his seat in Parliament in Boswell's favour, but when Montgomerie made no such commitment Boswell determined henceforth to work on his own for the Ayrshire seat. The death in February 1785 of James Erskine, who held the sinecure of Knight Marshal of Scotland, worth £400 a year, roused Boswell's hopes that he would get the position, and he wrote to Dundas accordingly; but Dundas replied that there were many applicants and Members of Parliament had the first option.

Unsuccessful in courting the powerful, Boswell now turned to opposition, and in June 1785, on the introduction by the Lord Advocate (now Sir Ilay Campbell) into the House of Commons of a Bill designed to cut down the number of judges in the Court of Session from fifteen to ten and increase the salaries of the remainder, he published a pamphlet entitled *A Letter to the People of Scotland, on the Alarming Attempt to infringe the Articles of the Union, and Introduce a most Pernicious Innovation, by diminishing the number of the Lords of Session*. His main argument was that the proposed measure was a violation of the Articles of Union, but he included lively sketches of important political characters, an attack on Dundas's domination of Scotland, reflections on the Ayrshire elections and an account of his own ancestry, friendships and ambitions. His criticism of Dundas was modified by acknowledgement of his abilities and of the friendship between the Boswell and Dundas families. He added: 'And I trust to the generosity of his feelings, that, as he *knows* he once did me a severe injury, which I have from my heart forgiven, he will be anxious to make me full amends, if ever it shall be in his power. The desire of elevation is as keen in me as in himself; though I am not so well fitted for party exploits.' Though the pamphlet was well received, and Boswell flattered himself that it was his 'persuasive and forcible' arguments that led to the Bill's being withdrawn, it nevertheless offended people on both sides and increased Boswell's political isolation.

Boswell arrived in London on 30 March 1785 to prepare his *Tour to the Hebrides* ('a good Prelude to my large Work his *Life*') for the press, but he spent a month in extravagant dining, wining and fornicating (not to mention visiting executions) before settling down to work, with the assiduous help of Malone, who suggested most of the changes that distinguish the published version from the manuscript. It was in London that he wrote the second *Letter to the People of Scotland*. He stayed in London right through the summer, working on the *Tour*, collecting materials for the *Life of Johnson* and having occasional fits of hypochondria and depression of spirits. At the same time, as he wrote John Johnston on 19 September, 'I have

(*Opposite*) The opening page of *The Journal of a Tour to the Hebrides*.

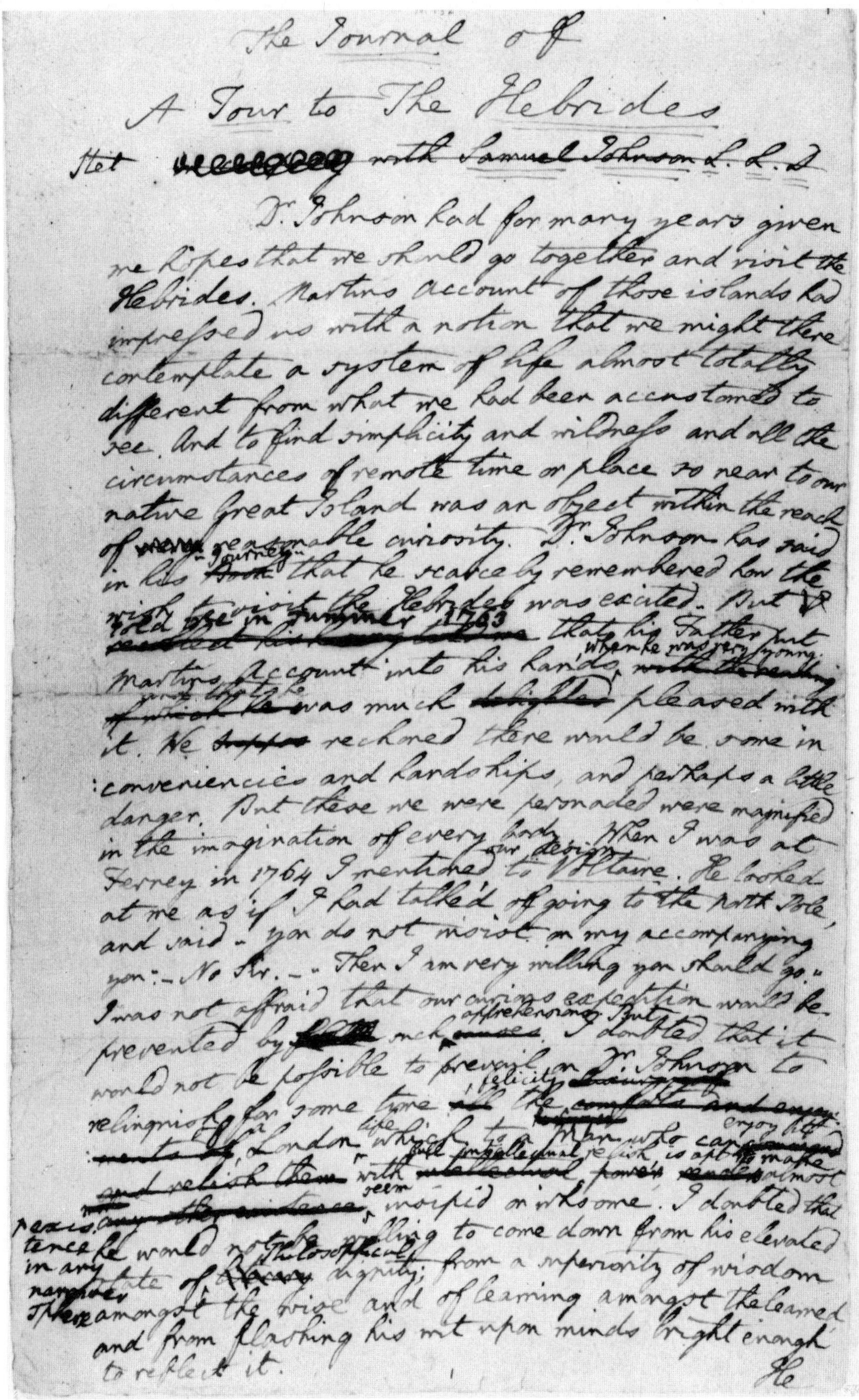

The Journal of

A Tour to The Hebrides

~~that~~ with Samuel Johnson L.L.D.

Dr. Johnson had for many years given me hopes that we should go together and visit the Hebrides. Martins account of those islands had impressed us with a notion that we might there contemplate a system of life almost totally different from what we had been accustomed to see. And to find simplicity and wildness and all the circumstances of remote time or place so near to our native great Island was an object within the reach of every reasonable curiosity. Dr. Johnson has said in his ~~Book~~ journey that he scarce by remembered how the wish to visit the Hebrides was excited. ~~But he told me in summer 1763~~ that his Father put Martins Account into his hands, when he was very young; and he was much ~~brighter~~ pleased with it. He ~~supposed~~ reckoned there would be some inconveniencies and hardships, and perhaps a little danger. But these we were persuaded were magnified in the imagination of every body. When I was at Ferney in 1764 I mentioned our design to Voltaire. He looked at me as if I had talked of going to the north Pole, and said - you do not insist on my accompanying you:- No Sir. - Then I am very willing you should go." I was not afraid that our curious expedition would be prevented by ~~such~~ objections. But I doubted that it would not be possible to prevail on Dr. Johnson to relinquish for some time ~~all the comfortable and easy~~ London, which to a Man who can enjoy it, is apt to make existence ~~seem~~ insipid or irksome. I doubted that he would not be willing to come down from his elevated ~~state of lofty dignity~~; from a superiority of wisdom amongst the wise and of learning amongst the learned and from flashing his wit upon minds bright enough to reflect it.

enjoyed such abundant happiness in this Place, since I saw you, that I declare I cannot help assimilating myself to one who had ascended into a superior state of existence.' He was back in Auchinleck by the beginning of October. He was in London again from 17 November to 22 December, which meant that he spent more than half of 1785 there. The fact is that he was thinking more and more seriously of settling in London. He consulted his friends endlessly on the subject, but in spite of their doubts about the wisdom of his action and his wife's pleadings against it, he took the plunge at the beginning of 1786. He left for London on 27 January and was called to the English Bar on 13 February. 'I . . . felt myself a Member of the ancient Court of King's Bench and did not despair of yet being a Judge in it. My mind was firm and serene, and my imagination bright.' He brought his wife and family to London in September.

The move to London meant throwing up his practice at the Scottish Bar and starting afresh at the English Bar at the age of forty-five. It was wholly unsuccessful. He obtained only one brief between February and November 1786. But, with no legal business to do, he was able to push ahead with the *Life of Johnson*. Day after day his Journal records how he worked first at sorting materials and then at writing. For three days in July he confined himself to the house (Great Queen Street, Lincoln's Inn Fields) 'and took only tea and dry toast to breakfast and boiled milk and dry toast at night' so as to be able to concentrate on the *Life*. Of course he also had his periods of indolence and ennui and his periodical distractions. But it must be emphasized that the *Life* required an enormous amount of sorting, arranging, planning and ordering, as well as the collection of information from a wide variety of sources and then the actual steady writing of the biography year by year, and Boswell did all this. He was unhappy away from his wife, but he thought it better for her health that she should stay at Auchinleck until she felt able to travel.

Boswell was now a briefless barrister, still hoping with increasing desperation for political office. In July 1786 he received an invitation to dinner from James Lowther, Earl of Lonsdale, an unscrupulous and powerful political manipulator with great influence in the north-west of England, where he had large estates. 'Jupiter' Carlyle called him 'a shameless political sharper, a domestic bashaw, and an intolerable tyrant over his tenants and dependents'. Boswell did not accept the dinner invitation (he had never met Lonsdale), but called on him formally and cautiously developed his acquaintance with the man of power. He was ready now to grasp at almost anything. He had written to Dundas to say he was willing to return to Scotland if he could get a judgeship, then again saying that since there was no vacancy on the Scottish Bench, he would like some job worth a few hundred pounds that would help him to live in London, but Dundas, when he finally replied, was still cool and non-committal.

Boswell's London house in Great Queen Street where he worked, a briefless barrister, on his *Life of Johnson*.

The General Assembly of the Kirk of Scotland 1787.

Lonsdale seemed the only hope, and by November Boswell was in a position to ask Lonsdale to make him Recorder of Carlisle (i.e. a judge having criminal and civil jurisdiction in the city), an appointment, like so many others in north-west England, that was in Lonsdale's pocket. Lonsdale offered Boswell instead the position of Mayor's Counsel at the forthcoming parliamentary election at Carlisle, and Boswell accepted. The rules of the borough required that only freemen (specifically, members of eight City Guilds) could vote, but Lonsdale had thought up the plan of creating 'honorary' freemen out of colliers and farmers not resident in the borough and enlisting them as voters on his side. Boswell, who had so vigorously attacked similar practices in Ayrshire, now found himself defending 'with animation and force' the right of the borough Corporation (which Lonsdale controlled) to make as many honorary freemen with the right to vote as they chose. Lonsdale's candidate won, but was unseated when his opponent petitioned the House of Commons. This was sad work for Boswell, but he could not afford to offend Lonsdale since he still hoped for the Recordership of Carlisle (regarded as a step to a seat in Parliament). In December 1787 Lonsdale finally offered him the Recordership. Boswell at first hesitated – after all, he now had fairly intimate knowledge of Lonsdale's

Boswell addressing the General Assembly of the Church of Scotland in 1787.

unpleasant character and realized that he was now permanently accepting him as his patron – and then accepted. Boswell set out for Carlisle with Lonsdale, increasingly aware that he was regarded as one of the arrogant Earl's hangers-on and thus increasingly unhappy with the appointment. He tried to withdraw, but Lonsdale dissuaded him, and on 11 January 1788 he was duly appointed Recorder. This did not mean that he gave up his hopes to represent Ayrshire in Parliament: on the contrary, he became more eager. He involved himself in a variety of political intrigues and then, when the sitting Member for Ayrshire, Montgomerie, was appointed Inspector of the Roads in North Britain in June 1789, a by-election in Ayrshire became inevitable, and Boswell calculated that by supporting the proper candidate he could ensure himself a seat at the next election. But his candidate did not get in, and he had to fall back on Lonsdale again.

It was in the midst of all this political activity that Mrs Boswell died. Boswell had had to go to London in May on Lonsdale's summons, while his wife was in Auchinleck. While there he received news that his wife, whom he had left very ill, had grown worse, and he hastened up to Ayrshire to find her dead on his arrival. He was bitterly self-reproachful, recalling how 'often and often when she was very ill in London have I been indulging in festivity with Sir Joshua Reynolds, Courtenay, Malone, etc., etc., and have come home late, and disturbed her repose. Nay, when I was last at Auchinleck on purpose to soothe and console her, I repeatedly went from home and both on those occasions, and when neighbours visited me, drank a great deal too much wine.'

Boswell was now often unhappy, sometimes dissipated, nearly always worried. He tried to persuade himself that Lonsdale was really a great man 'who upon any day that his fancy shall be so inclined may obtain for me an office which would make me independent'. He was now in his London house, which he much preferred to Carlisle. But in June 1790 Lonsdale insisted that Boswell go with him to Carlisle to fulfil his duties as Recorder at the election. In the carriage on the way north Boswell babbled about his 'liberal and independent views, and of their inconsistency with being brought in by him [Lonsdale] unless special terms were granted'. Lonsdale replied in 'shocking words', adding, 'You have kept low company all your life. What are *you*, Sir?' Boswell replied that he was a gentleman and a man of honour, and it looked as though a duel would be the only way out; but somehow the quarrel was made up. Boswell, however, was now aware that Lonsdale despised him as much as Boswell hated Lonsdale. He had already heard Lonsdale's reply to a suggestion from a third party that he should bring in Boswell as the Member for Carlisle: he could not do it because Boswell 'would get drunk and make a foolish speech'. When Boswell talked to Lonsdale of resigning the Recordership, Lonsdale, after telling him that he had no intention of bringing him into Parliament, made it clear that Boswell had sought the Recorder-ship and would have to do his duty by the office. In the end Boswell could stand it all no more, and wrote a formal letter of resignation on 23 June 1790. The 'irksome captivity' that involved him in 'low, dirty politicks' – as he wrote to his daughter Veronica – was too much. Lonsdale finally accepted his resignation on 15 July. 'I parted from the Northern Tyrant in a strange equivocal state,' he wrote Temple; 'for he was half irritated, half reconciled.' He promised Temple that he would keep himself henceforth quite independent of Lonsdale, and he did.

What could Boswell do now? Resume life as an advocate in Edin-burgh or a laird at Auchinleck? He could not bring himself to abandon his political hopes. 'It was generally assumed,' he wrote in the *European Magazine* article, 'that Mr. Boswell would have had a seat in Parliament; and indeed his not being amongst the representatives of the Commons is one of those strange things which occasionally happen in the complex operations of our mixed Government.' In the general election of July 1790 – again in his own words – 'he offered himself as a candidate . . . to represent Ayrshire, his own county, of which his is one of the oldest families, and where he has a very extensive property and a very fine place, . . . But the power of the Minister for Scotland was exerted for another person, and some of those whose support he might have expected could not withstand its influence; he therefore declined giving his friends the trouble of appearing for him; but he declared his resolution to persevere on the next vacancy.' His local Scottish pride was still working, geared to an obstinate and increasingly unrealistic hope of being able to represent his county at Westminster. When it was rumoured that the successful candidate was to get a place and vacate his seat, Boswell wrote passionately to Dundas protesting his own earlier services and invoking an earlier promise by Dundas (of which there is no record) to 'give me your interest to be member for my own County'. Dundas was not impressed. Boswell renewed his attempt to ingratiate himself with Pitt, which had been going on at intervals since 1784; Pitt had ignored a number of letters he had sent him asking to be allowed to wait on him. This time the approach was indirect and characteristic-ally Boswellian, and is best told in his words from the *European Magazine*. 'At the last Lord-Mayor's Day's festal board he sung with great applause a State Ballad of his own composition, entitled "The Grocer of London", in praise of Mr. Pitt's conduct in the dispute with Spain, a Convention being just then announced.' Boswell sang the ballad six times, but it has been suggested that Pitt (who attended the banquet) had left by the time Boswell started. At any rate, it made no impression on Pitt, who, Boswell wrote to Dundas the following week, '(I am utterly at a loss to know for what) has treated me arrogantly and ungratefully'.

The House of Lords, where Boswell appeared on behalf of a dismissed schoolmaster in 1772, and whose procedure and status as the ultimate Appeal Court of the land continued to fascinate him.

William Pitt, the Grocer of London was printed in November, first in London and then in *The Edinburgh Advertiser*. Boswell's next publication was a curious poem entitled *No Abolition of Slavery; or, The Universal Empire of Love* in which he combined an ingeniously paradoxical defence of the slave-trade (a Bill to abolish which had just been introduced into Parliament), lively references to his friends, praise of Pitt and of Thurlow the Lord Chancellor and a profession of love for a lady conjecturally identified as a Miss Bagnal, one of several ladies he cheered himself by considering as a possible second wife. 'But' (to continue with Boswell's own account) 'his attention to the business of Westminster-Hall has been chiefly interrupted by his great literary work in which he was engaged for many years, *The*

Life of Dr. Johnson, which has at last been published, in two volumes quarto, and which has been received by the world with extraordinary approbation.'

Boswell had finished the *Life* under very gloomy conditions. After his wife's death and his unsuccessful intervention in the Ayrshire election of 1789 he had returned from Auchinleck to London, with all his children except Euphemia, who was now at a boarding-school in Edinburgh, to occupy a rented house in Queen Anne Street West (which was conveniently near Malone). There, and at 122 Great Portland Street where he moved in January 1791, he forced the work along, with the usual intervals of depression, drunkenness and dissipation. With Malone at his elbow to keep him at it and to argue him

A cartoonist's impression of lawyers in Westminster Hall. Called to the English Bar in 1786, Boswell felt himself 'a Member of the ancient Court of King's Bench and did not despair of yet being a Judge in it'.

drawn April 28th 1793   JAMES BOSWELL ESQr

out of his frequent moods of discouragement, he organized material, wrote, revised. 'You cannot imagine what labour, what perplexity, what vexation I have endured in arranging a prodigious multiplicity of materials, in supplying omissions, in searching for papers buried in different masses – and all this besides the exertion of composing and polishing,' he wrote to Temple on 30 November 1789. But though the work might at times seem like drudgery, in intention, design, liveliness and dramatic force it showed Boswell's controlling conception of biography. Brilliant and memorable though Johnson's recorded conversations so often are, their illuminating power derives from the fact that Boswell displayed them in the light of his own imaginatively and intellectually conceived concept of Johnson's moral and literary character, deepened by real research. Paradoxically, Boswell's narcissism helped to make him a brilliant observer of others. He used himself as a means of striking sparks off Johnson. Above all, a relentless human curiosity pushed him forward, not only to observe and record in as vivid and lifelike a way as possible, but also to keep on questioning, wondering, speculating on the why and the how and the whether of his hero's behaviour.

The enthusiastic reception of his *Life of Johnson* cheered Boswell, but did not solve his problems. He wrote to his friends and his children about them and discussed them in his Journal. 'I was in truth in a woeful state of depression in every respect. The animating delusion that I might get practice in Westminster-Hall had vanished; for I saw plainly that all my habits and appearances in publick were, as Malone well observed, against me as a Lawyer; and I was conscious that I had never applied seriously to English Law, and could not bear the confinement and formal course of life which Practice at the bar required. I yet shrunk from the thought of returning to my seat in the country, and considered that as my profession was *Jurisconsultus*, it would be a sad thing to abandon it.' A final flare-up of his political hopes occurred after the Corsicans revolted against France in 1793 and announced their willingness to be annexed to Great Britain. Britain sent troops to the island and Boswell, who had reason to consider himself the great Corsican expert in the country, wrote to Dundas asking for the post of Minister to Corsica or Royal Commissioner there; the reply was a 'cold ministerial letter' telling him that Sir Gilbert Elliot of Minto was in charge of Corsican affairs and had no need of Boswell's services. Now, 'finding no prospect of attaining my ambitious objects, I tried to soothe myself with the consideration of my fame as a Writer, and that by the good management of my Estate, and saving, I might in time pay my debts.' He wrote his son James in November 1794: 'I will try to avoid repining. Yet at the same time, I cannot be contented merely with literary fame, and social enjoyments. I must still hope for some credible employment; and perhaps I may yet attain to it.'

(*Opposite*) The Laird of Auchinleck, barrister, author and celebrity.

So he persisted in hoping, or at least in pretending to himself that he was hoping. He stayed on in London; 'the best place when one is happy, it is equally so when one is the reverse'; drank more and more, tried to stifle pangs of solitude with wild debauches and nocturnal adventures. He had by now lost all credibility as a responsible candidate for significant political office: his irresponsibility, intemperance, exhibitionism and changeableness of mood were widely known. Yet he was liked. He could still set the table in a roar, entertain with a song or a witticism, abandon himself to the social hour with attractive liveliness. But he had really nothing more to do. Of all the alternative Boswells with which he had entertained his fancy since his early years – the glitteringly uniformed Guards officer, the peaceful and well-loved Scottish laird, the brilliant Court wit, the great parliamentarian – it was as diarist and, more especially, as biographer that he truly found himself. All his life he had been in search of Boswell. What he was never to realize was that the search turned him into a great biographer of others as well as a great recorder of himself. When he died, after a short illness, at his London house in Great Portland Street on 19 May 1795 he had not discovered that his search for his true identity was over.

1740 29 October: Boswell born in Edinburgh

1746 attends James Mundell's school

1748 or 1749 leaves Mundell's and begins education by private tutors

1752 serious illness and recovery at Moffat

1753 autumn: begins attendance at Edinburgh University

1757 melancholia, 'Methodism', and second visit to Moffat

1758 October: begins study of law. Becomes involved with the stage and actresses

1759 sent to Glasgow University. His first publication, *A View of the Edinburgh Theatre*

1760 March: runs away to London. June: returns to Auchinleck to study law with his father

1762 30 July: passed examination in Civil Law. Autumn: 'Harvest Jaunt'. His first Journal

1762–63 in London

1763 16 May: first meeting with Johnson

1763 (August)–1764 (June) in Holland

1764 June–November: tour in Germany. December: visits to Rousseau and Voltaire

1765 January–October: in Italy. October–November: visit to Corsica

1766 March: returns to Scotland after a stay in Paris and in London. July: passes examination in Scots law and 'passes advocate'

1767 becomes involved in the Douglas cause. 15 June: *Dorando* published. August: *The Essence of the Douglas Cause* published

1768 18 February: *Account of Corsica* published. March–June: in London. December: *British Essays in Favour of the Brave Corsicans* published

1768–69 in search of a wife

1769 August: becomes engaged to his cousin, Margaret Montgomerie. September–November: in London. September: attends Shakespeare Jubilee at Stratford. 25 November: marries Margaret Montgomerie at Lainshaw

1772 19 March–8 May: in London

1773 August–October: tour with Johnson to the Hebrides

1774 August: John Reid's trial

1775 21 March–22 May: in London

1776 15 March–16 May: in London

1777 September: visit to see Johnson at Ashbourne. October: begins writing the 'Hypochondriack' essays for *The London Magazine*

1778 17 March–28 May: in London

1779 15 March–3 May: in London. October: in London again

1781 19 March–5 June: in London and Southill

1782 30 August: death of Lord Auchinleck

1783 20 March–30 May: in London. Publication of *A Letter to the People of Scotland on the Present State of the Nation*

1784 March: sets out for London but turns back at York on learning of the dissolution of Parliament. 5 May–30 June: in London. Sees Johnson for the last time. 13 December: death of Johnson

1785 publishes *A Letter to the People of Scotland on the Alarming Attempt to infringe the Articles of the Union . . . by diminishing the number of the Lords of Session.* More than half of this year in London, preparing *Tour of the Hebrides* for the press and collecting material for *Life of Johnson*

1786 January: settles in London. 13 February: called to the English Bar. July: begins association with Lord Lonsdale

1788 11 January: appointed Recorder of Carlisle

1789 June: death of Mrs Boswell. June–August: unsuccessful involvement in Ayrshire by-election

1790 June: resigns Recordership of Carlisle and breaks association with Lonsdale. July: unsuccessful attempt to stand as candidate for Ayrshire in general election

1791 16 May: publication of *Life of Johnson*

1795 19 May: death in London

BIBLIOGRAPHICAL NOTE

The special circumstances of Boswell's bibliography require an explanatory note rather than a 'select bibliography'. The recovery of vast numbers of Boswell papers in the present century – first from Malahide Castle in 1926, then from Fettercairn in 1930, then again from Malahide Castle in 1937, 1939 and 1948 – and their eventual acquisition by Yale University revealed the full nature of Boswell's extraordinary self-documentation in journals, diaries, letters and memoranda, as well as the original manuscripts of both the *Life of Johnson* and the *Journal of the Tour to the Hebrides*. A limited edition of the *Private Papers of James Boswell from Malahide Castle* was privately printed in New York between 1928 and 1934 in eighteen volumes, the first six edited by Geoffrey Scott and the remaining twelve by F. A. Pottle. An index volume was published in 1937. Later, a group of scholars at Yale, under the chairmanship of F. A. Pottle, planned two editions of the Yale Boswell papers, a 'research' edition and a 'reading' or 'trade' edition.

The two volumes of the research edition so far published are:

The Correspondence of James Boswell and John Johnston of Grange, edited by R. S. Walker. New Haven, Conn., and London, 1966.

The Correspondence and Other Papers of James Boswell relating to the Making of the 'Life of Johnson', edited by Marshall Waingrow. New Haven, Conn., and London, 1969.

The following volumes have so far appeared in the trade edition:

Boswell's London Journal, 1762–1763, edited by F. A. Pottle. New York and London, 1950.

Boswell in Holland, 1763–1764, edited by F. A. Pottle. New York and London, 1952.

Boswell on the Grand Tour: Germany and Switzerland, 1764, edited by F. A. Pottle. New York and London, 1953.

Boswell on the Grand Tour: Italy, Corsica and France, 1765–1766, edited by F. A. Pottle. New York and London, 1954.

Boswell in Search of a Wife, 1766–1769, edited by Frank Brady and F. A. Pottle. New York and London, 1957.

Boswell for the Defence, 1769–1774, edited by W. K. Wimsatt and F. A. Pottle. New York and London, 1960.

Boswell: the Ominous Years, 1774–1776, edited by Charles Ryskamp and F. A. Pottle. New York and London, 1963.

Boswell in Extremes, 1776–1778, edited by C. McC. Weis and F. A. Pottle. New York and London, 1971.

The following are editions of works by Boswell:

The Journal of a Tour to Corsica; and Memoirs of Pascal Paoli, by James Boswell, Esq., edited by M. Bishop. London, 1951.

Boswell's Column, Being his Seventy Contributions to the London Magazine, edited by Margaret Bailey. London, 1931.

Johnson's Tour to the Western Islands of Scotland and Boswell's Journal of a Tour to the Hebrides with Samuel Johnson, LL.D., edited by R. W. Chapman, London, 1930.

Boswell's Journal of a Tour to the Hebrides with Samuel Johnson, LL.D. Now First Published from the Original Manuscript, edited by F. A. Pottle and C. H. Bennett. New York and London, 1936.

The Life of Samuel Johnson, LL.D. edited by G. Birbeck Hill, revised by L. F. Powell. Six vols. Oxford, 1934–40.

Letters of James Boswell, addressed to the Rev. W. J. Temple, edited by T. Seccombe. London, 1908.

Letters of James Boswell, edited by C. B. Tinker. Two vols. London, 1924.

The following are books about Boswell or his background:

Frank Brady, *Boswell's Political Career*. New Haven and London, 1965.

Mary Hyde, *The Impossible Friendship: Boswell and Mrs. Thrale*. Cambridge, Mass., and London, 1973.

F. A. Pottle, *The Literary Career of James Boswell, Esq.* Oxford and New York 1965.

F. A. Pottle, *James Boswell: The Earlier Years, 1740–1769*. New York and London, 1966.

Ayrshire at the Time of Burns. Ayrshire Archaeological and Natural History Society, 1959. (Contains, among other things, Boswell's Election Address 'to the Real Freeholders of the County of Ayr', 17 March 1784).

LIST OF ILLUSTRATIONS

Credit line in italics indicates that the photograph was provided by the named museum or other institution.

34–5 Extract from James Boswell's *London Journal* recording his first meeting with Samuel Johnson on Monday, 16 May 1763. *Yale University Library.*

36 The Cock Tavern. Pen and wash drawing by Thomas Rowlandson. Gilbert Davies, Esq., London.

37 In the Mall. Pen and wash drawing by Thomas Rowlandson. *Courtesy of the Trustees of the British Museum.* .

38 View of Harwich. Eighteenth-century engraving by R. Sheppard. *British Library.*

39 View of Leiden. Eighteenth-century engraving. *British Library.*

40 View of the Haringvliet in the city of Rotterdam. Engraving by L. Brasfer, 1762. *British Library.*

41 View of the City Hall in The Hague. Engraving by H. Scheurleer, 1760. *British Library.*

43 Portrait of Belle de Zuylen (1740–1805). Oil on canvas by Jens Juel, *c.* 1777. Photo Iconographisch Bureau, The Hague. Collection Stichting Kasteel Zuylen.

45 The Royal Palace, Berlin. Engraving by J. Rosenberg, 1781. *Courtesy of the Trustees of the British Museum.*

46 Portrait of Jean-Jacques Rousseau. Oil on canvas by Allan Ramsay, 1766. National Gallery of Scotland.

L'Embarquement des Lapins, illustration from *Les Confessions* by Jean-Jacques Rousseau, showing Rousseau, Thérèse, his dog Sultan, with the Receiver's wife and sister, taking rabbits to inhabit a tiny island south of the Île Saint-Pierre on the Lac de Bienne. Late eighteenth-century engraving by N. Monsiaux. *Bibliothèque Nationale, Paris.*

47 Voltaire. Etching of a caricature by Jean Huber.

48 The Arrival of a Young Traveller and his Suite in the Piazza di Spagna, Rome. Drawing by David Allan (1744–96). Reproduced by gracious permission of Her Majesty the Queen.

49 John Wilkes. Detail from a satirical print, *c.* 1763–67. *Courtesy of the Trustees of the British Museum.*

50 View of Siena. Eighteenth-century etching. *British Library.*

51 Portrait of James Boswell. Oil on canvas by George Willison, 1765. Scottish National Portrait Gallery.

53 Pasquale Paoli. Engraving by C. Bowles after portrait by Bembridge. Dr Johnson's House, Gough Square.

The badge worn by the followers of General Paoli given to James Boswell. Dr Johnson's House, Gough Square.

55 Portrait of William Pitt, first Earl of Chatham (1708–78). After R. Brompton. *National Portrait Gallery, London.*

57 Portrait of Mrs Boswell. Painting attributed to George Willison. Photo National Portrait Gallery, London. Hyde Collection, Somerville, New Jersey.

59 The Old Tolbooth, Edinburgh. Engraving after Alexander Nasmyth. *By courtesy of Edinburgh City Library.*

60 Portrait of Henry Dundas, first Viscount Melville (1742–1811). Painting by T. Lawrence. *National Portrait Gallery, London.*

61 Portrait of Archibald Douglas, first Baron Douglas. Mezzotint by Valentine Green after George Willison, 1770. By kind permission of the Duke of Hamilton.

63 John Wilkes Esq., before the Court of King's Bench, 20th April 1762. Satirical engraving. *Courtesy of the Trustees of the British Museum.*

64 Portrait of David Hume. Painting by Allan Ramsay. National Gallery of Scotland.

65 Portrait of Samuel Johnson. Painting by Joshua Reynolds, 1756. *National Portrait Gallery, London.*

67 Portrait of James Boswell in the dress of a Corsican Chief. Engraving by J. Miller, *c.* 1770. *National Portrait Gallery, London.*

68 Mr Thrale's House, Streatham. Engraving by E. Finden after C. Stanfield.

69 Portrait of Hester Thrale. Engraving by E. Finden after Joshua Reynolds.

70 View of the High Street of Edinburgh and the Commissioner going to the General Assembly of the Kirk of Scotland. Hand-coloured etching by David Allan, 1793. National Gallery of Scotland.

71 Portrait of Dr Goldsmith. Engraving by J. Bretherton after H. Bunbury. Dr Johnson's House, Gough Square.

72 Letter from Johnson to Goldsmith, proposing Boswell as a

member of The Club, 1773. Dr Johnson's House, Gough Square.

73 Johnson, Goldsmith and Boswell at the Mitre Tavern, Fleet Street. Engraving by R.B. Parkes after the painting by Eyre Crowe.

74 The Embrace. From *The Picturesque Beauties of Boswell*, 1786, etched by Thomas Rowlandson after designs by Samuel Collings. By courtesy of the Victoria and Albert Museum.

75 Walking up the High Street. From *The Picturesque Beauties of Boswell*, 1786, etched by Thomas Rowlandson after designs by Samuel Collings.

76 Portree on the Isle of Skye. Aquatint by William Daniell, from Ayton's *Voyage around Great Britain*, published 1819. *Courtesy of the Trustees of the British Museum.*

77 The Visit of Dr Johnson and James Boswell to Flora Macdonald. Painting. Dr Johnson's House, Gough Square.

78-9 Tea; Setting out from Edinburgh; Sailing among the Hebrides; The Procession; The Dance on Duncan; The Recovery. From *The Picturesque Beauties of Boswell*, 1786, etched by Thomas Rowlandson after designs by Samuel Collings. By courtesy of the Victoria and Albert Museum.

80 Johnson in Travelling Dress as described in Boswell's *Journal of a Tour to the Hebrides*. Engraving by T. Trotter. *Courtesy of the Trustees of the British Museum.*

81 The Contest at Auchinleck. From *The Picturesque Beauties of Boswell*, 1786, etched by Thomas Rowlandson after designs by Samuel Collings.

83 The Journalist. From *The Picturesque Beauties of Boswell*, 1786, etched by Thomas Rowlandson after designs by Samuel Collings. By courtesy of the Victoria and Albert Museum.

85 Portrait of James Boswell with his family. Painting by Henry Singleton. Scottish National Portrait Gallery.

86 Portrait of General Paoli. Engraving by Cardon after Guttenbrun. By courtesy of the Victoria and Albert Museum.

View of the Temple from the River, c. 1790. Watercolour by an unknown artist. Courtesy of the Trustees of the London Museum.

87 Portrait of Hester Piozzi (formerly Thrale) (1741-1821). Drawing by George Dance. *National Portrait Gallery, London.*

88 A Scene in Islington Fields, 1773. Satirical engraving by Walker Fitzgerald. *Courtesy of the Trustees of the British Museum.*

89 Dr Johnson's house, Bolt Court, Fleet Street. Engraving by S. Rawle after Shepherd, published 1810. *Courtesy of the Trustees of the British Museum.*

91 Portrait of James Boswell. Painting by Joshua Reynolds, 1785. *National Portrait Gallery, London.*

92 The Meadows, Edinburgh, c. 1810. Engraving from J. Grant's *Old and New Edinburgh. By courtesy of Edinburgh City Library.*

93 Ashbourne Church, Derbyshire. Engraving by E. Finden after C. Stanfield. *National Monuments Record.*

94 Contents page of *The London Magazine*, November 1782, showing 'The Hypochondriack's' entry. *British Library.*

96 A Literary Party at Sir Joshua Reynolds' house, with Boswell, Johnson, Reynolds, Garrick, Burke, Paoli, Burney, Warton and Goldsmith. Engraving by W. Walker after James E. Doyle. Dr Johnson's House, Gough Square.

97 Self-Portrait as President of the Royal Academy of Arts. Painting by Joshua Reynolds. *Royal Academy of Arts, London.*

Portrait of Samuel Johnson. Painting by John Opie. Photo National Galleries of Scotland. Reproduced by kind permission of the Earl of Crawford and Balcarres.

99 View of Edinburgh. Aquatint by John Wells after R. Barker, from *Panoramic Views of the City of Edinburgh*, 1790. *British Library.*

100 The Right Honourable Robert Dundas, Lord President of the Court of Session. Engraving by William Sharp, published 1790. By courtesy of the Victoria and Albert Museum.

The first Viscount Melville. Painting by Henry Raeburn, c. 1804. *Tate Gallery.*

101 'A London Chop House', with caricatures of Johnson and Boswell. Engraving by H. Bunbury, published 1781. *Courtesy of the Trustees of the British Museum.*

102-3 Letter from James Boswell to Bennet Langton, written from Edinburgh, 20 February 1778. Dr Johnson's House, Gough Square.

105 Bozzy . . . Madame Piozzi. Satirical engraving by Thomas Rowlandson, 1786. *Courtesy of the Trustees of the British Museum.*

106 The Late Lord Melville and the Present Lord Chief Baron. Etching No. 162 (1790) from John Kay's *Edinburgh Portraits. Courtesy of the Trustees of the British Museum.*

107 Execution at Newgate. Ink and watercolour by Thomas Rowlandson. *Courtesy of the Trustees of the London Museum.*

109 Opening page of the manuscript of Boswell's *Life of Johnson. Yale University Library.*

111 Opening page of the manuscript of Boswell's *Journal of a Tour to the Hebrides. Yale University Library.*

112 Boswell's house, Great Queen Street. Drawing by F. L. Emanuel. Courtesy of the Trustees of the London Museum.

113 Boswell orating to the General Assembly of the Church of Scotland in the Tron Church, Edinburgh. Pen and wash, 1787. *British Library.*

116 The House of Lords. Aquatint by Thomas Rowlandson. By courtesy of the Victoria and Albert Museum.

117 Term Time, or The Lawyers All Alive in Westminster Hall. Hand-coloured mezzotint, published 1797. By permission of F. E. Smith, Esq., of Gray's Inn.

118 Portrait of James Boswell. Drawing by George Dance, 1793. *Courtesy of the Trustees of the British Museum.*

INDEX

Page numbers in italics refer to illustrations